BEING RESILIENT

50 Lessons on Leaving Chronic Stress Behind

Adam Timm
Joe Serio, Ph.D.

Copyright © 2017

No part of this publication may be transmitted in any form or by any means, electronic, mechanical, photocopying, recording, scanning, or by an information storage and retrieval system, or otherwise, except as permitted under Sections 107 or 108 of the 1976 U.S. Copyright Act, without the prior written consent of the Publisher.

This publication is designed to provide accurate and authoritative information in regard to the subject matter covered. It is sold with the understanding that neither the Author nor the Publisher is engaged in rendering legal, accounting, financial or other professional services. If legal advice or other expert assistance is required, the services of a competent professional should be sought. Neither the Publisher nor the Author shall be liable for damages, directly or indirectly, arising herefrom.

Design Team: Harriet McHale and Tracey Neikirk

Printed in the United States of America
ISBN 13: 978-0-9987240-9-6

www.joeserio.com

Contents

ABOUT THE GET THE NERVE™ SERIES ... 7

INTRODUCTION ... 10

PART 1
BURNT ... 13

Lesson 1:	Burnout	14
Lesson 2:	The Nature of the Beast	16
Lesson 3:	Forms of Daily Stress	18
Lesson 4:	Feeling the Effects	20
Lesson 5:	Julia's Story	22
Lesson 6:	The Type A Personality	24
Lesson 7;	What Happens at Home?	26
Lesson 8:	My Realization	28

PART 2
MAKING THE MENTAL SHIFT ... 31

Lesson 9:	The Paradigm Shift	32
Lesson 10:	Your Beliefs Define Your Perspective	34
Lesson 11:	The Gap between Belief and Reality	36
Lesson 12:	Values: Knowing What's Important	38
Lesson 13:	Priorities: Doing What's Important	40
Lesson 14:	Looking Deeper	42
Lesson 15:	E + R = O	44
Lesson 16:	Fight or Flight...or the Third Way	46
Lesson 17:	Choose the Story of Your Life Wisely	48

MAY – 2023

Lesson 18:	The Warning Signs	50
Lesson 19:	Make Your Relationships Work for You	52
Lesson 20:	Taking Charge of Your Life	54

PART 3
INSIDE YOUR BRAIN 55

Lesson 21:	Laura Makes the Transition	56
Lesson 22:	Destination Relaxation	60
Lesson 23:	Relaxation Techniques	62
Lesson 24:	Slow Yourself Down	64
Lesson 25:	No More Avoidance	66
Lesson 26:	Cultivating Resilience	68
Lesson 27:	What You Focus On Expands	70
Lesson 28;	Change the Changeable	72
Lesson 29:	Do One Thing at a Time	74

PART 4
AVOIDING THE TRAPS 77

Lesson 30:	Stay Out of Your Thinking Traps	78
Lesson 31:	The Daily Thought Record	80
Lesson 32:	Silence Your Inner Critic	82
Lesson 33:	You Can If You Think You Can	84
Lesson 34:	Know the Power of Your Will	86
Lesson 35:	Letting Go of the Hassles	88

PART 5
MAKING THE PHYSICAL SHIFT 91

| Lesson 36: | Eliminate the Stress-Promoting Diet | 92 |
| Lesson 37: | Reduce Your Stress with Exercise | 94 |

| Lesson 38: | Be a Sleeping Beauty | 96 |
| Lesson 39: | Laugh Whenever You Can | 98 |

PART 6
LIVING YOUR NEW REALITY — 101

Lesson 40:	With a Little Help from My Friends	102
Lesson 41:	To Forgive is to Get Something Back	104
Lesson 42:	Don't Take Work Home	106
Lesson 43:	Get a Life	108
Lesson 44:	Re-discovery	110
Lesson 45:	Seeing the Connection	112
Lesson 46:	Lisa Makes the Connection	114

PART 7
CREATING YOUR FUTURE — 117

Lesson 47:	The Vision for Tomorrow	118
Lesson 48:	One Step at a Time	120
Lesson 49:	You Know the Way	122
Lesson 50:	Celebrate the Journey	124

THE ROAD AHEAD — 126

THE TAKEAWAYS — 128

ACKNOWLEDGMENTS — 133

BIOGRAPHY — 135

The long span of the bridge of your life is supported by countless cables called habits, attitudes, and desires. What you do in life depends upon what you are and what you want. What you get from life depends upon how much you want it, how much you are willing to work and plan and cooperate and use your resources. The long span of the bridge of your life is supported by countless cables that you are spinning now, and that is why today is such an important day. Make the cables strong!

~ L.G. Elliott

About the *Get the Nerve™ Series*

The idea for the *Get the Nerve™ Series* grew out of my personal transformation from being fearful of most things to facing that fear and achieving more than I thought possible.

My goal is to share what I and others have learned so that you, too, can see the possibility for your own life and make it a reality.

As L.G. Elliott says in the quotation on the facing page, "Your life is supported by countless cables called habits, attitudes, and desires." This series is a blueprint for helping you create and strengthen the cables of your bridge so you can live the most inspired life you can imagine.

I would love to hear about changes you make in your life as a result of the *Get the Nerve™ Series*. Please contact me with your stories of personal transformation at joe@joeserio.com.

Joe Serio, Ph.D.

Other Titles in the *Get the Nerve™ Series*

Overcoming Fear: 50 Lessons on Being Bold and Living the Dream

Time Management: 50 Lessons on Finding Time for What's Important

Public Speaking: 50 Lessons on Presenting Without Losing Your Cool

Effective Communication: 50 Lessons on How to Hear and Be Heard

Leadership: 50 Lessons on Inspiring Others to Be Their Best

Emotional Intelligence: 50 Lessons on Knowing Who You're Dealing With

Introduction

For, usually and fitly, the presence of an introduction is held to imply that there is something of consequence and importance to be introduced.
~ Arthur Machen

I'm very pleased to have Adam Timm as the primary author on this title in the Get the Nerve™ series of books. I had the good fortune to be in Los Angeles for a conference a few years ago.

I approached the registration table and started a conversation with the conference staff member. She asked me my background and I told her about my wellness trainings for law enforcement. She exclaimed, "You have to meet my friend, Adam! He's a 911 dispatcher at the LAPD."

Fortunately, I was wise enough to heed her advice, and Adam and I met during my stay in LA.

At that time, I had been delivering wellness and life skills classes to law enforcement agencies around Texas. In talking with dispatchers at those programs, I learned that there was very little offered by way of wellness training specifically for dispatchers. The thought to create classes was already in my mind when Adam and I met.

Later, we piloted de-stress classes for dispatchers in Austin, Ft. Worth, Denton, and Houston. The class was incredibly well received.

Since then, Adam and I have launched several classes for 911 dispatchers, including De-stress and Get More Me Time; Positive Interaction with Difficult People; and Transformational Leadership.

Adam and I are delighted to be able to present you with this book. It was originally written as *Dispatcher Stress: 50 Lessons on Beating the Burnout*. It got such rave reviews that we decided to edit it for a general audience. Our goal for readers, though, is still the same: to help you get more of what you want out of life.

Here's the thing about the material in this book: It works!

Both Adam and I have come from places of fear, stress, anger, anxiety, and exhaustion. We had toxic relationships, road rage, and insomnia. We were definitely not getting what we wanted out of life.

On our separate paths, we used similar techniques as each other to arrive at the same place. Those techniques are outlined in this book.

As with any material of this type, the secret to your success is in the doing. You can read this book, buy other books, watch videos, or talk to people, but until you actually step into action, nothing will happen.

Trust the process, take it step by step, and begin to bring meaningful change to your life.

The choice is always yours. In fact, your life as you know it today is based largely on the choices you've made to this point. You can change your choices, you can change your mind, anytime you want.

How to Use This Book

Part 1, Burnt, provides an overview of the challenges you face day in and day out in your job, as well as in life as a wife, husband, mother, father, sister, brother, son, or daughter.

Part 2, Making the Mental Shift, lays out the foundation of change. This material is invaluable for assessing where you are and how to move into a different future.

Part 3, Steps to Reducing Your Stress, is the heart of the techniques to reduce your stress and bring change to your life immediately.

Part 4, Avoiding the Traps, acknowledges that sometimes the road can be difficult and so presents information and techniques for minimizing obstacles in your path to change.

Part 5, Making the Physical Shift, focuses on the relationship between your body and your stress, highlighting the need for proper diet, exercise, sleep, and laughter.

Part 6, Living Your New Reality, is about lightening up and actually putting into practice the things that make you happy and keep you engaged with the people in your life.

Part 7, Creating Your Future, is primarily about trusting yourself. Everything you need is inside you once you get past the fear and apprehension of moving forward.

While you could read *Being Resilient* in any order, I recommend reading it from beginning to end. There is an arc, a logical progression, to the lessons.

The benefits you will get from reading—and applying—the lessons in this book cannot be fully described. You must experience it. You will see shifts you never thought possible. You will gain perspective you've never had. You will notice improvement in virtually every area of your life. But it's up to you. No one else can do it for you.

In a nutshell, this book is about you. Everything you need to start addressing your stress is inside you. The lessons we've laid out will help you bring those things out. If you find this process easy, you're probably not doing it right. You will have to ask some difficult questions of yourself and face some painful realities. That's OK. That's normal. But the work is doable, and it's worth it.

Master the lessons in this book and you will become more resilient and change your life.

Part 1

Burnt

Lesson 1
Burnout

If stress burned calories, I'd be a supermodel.
~ Unknown

I have a theory that burnout is about resentment. And you beat it by knowing what it is you're giving up that makes you resentful.
~ Marissa Mayer

Welcome to your stressful life. Who knew it would be like this? It seems like everywhere you turn, there's another layer. There's stress waking up on time, stress on the morning commute, stress at work, stress at home, and, if you've got a second job like so many of us, there's stress there, too.

This is especially the case if you find yourself a caregiver to the world. You're the person people rely on. You're the one willing to stay late. You're the one who's always helping others.

And it's not only on the job. Have you ever tried to sit still on your day off and found it nearly impossible? The only thing you can do is think about the next thing you have to do…or maybe you just sit there, feeling anxious…or feeling any of the many other pains that stress brings about for you.

Over time, you learn that your big heart and desire to help everyone and to live up to everyone's expectations can expose you to a new challenge: burnout. Burnout is the state of emotional, mental, and physical exhaustion caused by excessive and prolonged stress. It occurs when you feel overwhelmed and unable to meet constant demands. As the stress continues, you begin to lose the interest or motivation that led you to take your role in the first place.

That's when you begin to feel like you have no real control over your job. You feel that what you do has little effect. You feel that people who aren't experiencing your world couldn't possibly understand. You start looking at your job with an attitude of "What's the use?" The job isn't as much fun as it used to be.

This leads to frustration and later resignation. You don't *actually* resign, though. You just do the absolute minimum to get by. You hide from the prospect of extra duty. You use your sick time regularly and complain about the morale problem (even though you contribute to it). Does any of this sound familiar?

I blamed my feelings of burnout on everyone else for years before taking responsibility for the way I was feeling.

The moment I chose to do something differently, a new path emerged.

Burnout is an opportunity. It's an opportunity to explore the thoughts and expectations that brought you to that moment. It's an opportunity to take better care of yourself, to take time to have more fun.

Like anything that happens in your life, you can choose to learn from it and do something about it, or you can keep doing the same things over and over expecting different results.

Wherever you are right now is the perfect place to start. As you'll soon see, a small amount of effort, expended each day for the next few weeks, can deliver you to a completely different place.

TAKEAWAY: Burnout happens when you suppress your feelings and expect things to change without doing something different. So do something different.

Lesson 2
The Nature of the Beast

There is no stress in the world,
only people thinking stressful thoughts.
～ Dr. Wayne Dyer

Our greatest weapon against stress is
our ability to choose one thought over another.
～ William James

Burnout creeps up after years of feeling stressed. Many factors—some controllable, others not—combine to leave you strung out, tense, sometimes bitter, and exhausted.

There's the workday: meeting deadlines, demanding clients, demanding bosses, a negative work environment, poor communication—and you haven't even gotten to lunch yet!

Then there's what happens after. You have your home life to tend to, which, depending on the day, can feel more challenging than things at work ever do: sick kids, bills, child care, chores, traffic...you know the drill.

It all adds up as layer after layer gets heaped on top of you.

You might not think you're stressed. You might think you have it all under control.

Until someone says something and...you snap!

This stress cycle—the build-up, then release—becomes such a regular part of life that you think this is just how it is. You spend so much of your day locked in this cycle that you might even believe you need to feel stressed to be at your best.

When asked if he wanted to participate in a de-stress workshop, a gentleman I met at a recent speaking event said, "No thanks. I wouldn't want to lose my edge."

While a short burst of stress does tune you up in the heat of the moment, ongoing feelings of stress, each and every day, do more harm than good.

Sixty percent of all doctor visits are stress-related, and chronic stress is linked to six of the leading causes of death!

The chronically stressed are more accident prone, more easily frustrated and confused, and aren't as happy as their less-stressed friends.

It may seem that daily life and chronic stress go hand-in-hand—that one cannot exist without the other. But what if this weren't true? What if you could lower your stress levels and be a better parent, spouse, child, or sibling?

Recent research has shown a link between less stress and better memory, better sleep, and greater regulation of your emotional state. With less stress, there's more happy!

The challenge, then, is to untangle your daily life from the old stressful thoughts and choose thoughts that aren't so stressful. When you do this, it's a game-changer. This book will show you how.

TAKEAWAY: Burnout is driven by the stress cycles of your daily life.

Lesson 3
Forms of Daily Stress

*The life you have led doesn't need to be
the only life you have.*
~ Anna Quindlen

*A diamond is just a piece of charcoal that handled
stress exceptionally well.*
~ Unknown

After years of working and perhaps raising a family, daily stressors and their effects are just a normal part of the day. It's like the story of the boiling frog.

The myth goes, if you put a live frog in a pot of cold water, put that pot on a stovetop burner, and turn the heat to low, the frog will adjust to the temperature of the water and be fine. Turn the heat to medium and the frog will adjust to the temperature and still be just fine. Turn the heat to high and the frog continues to adjust until the water begins to boil. Then what happens? Yep. The frog dies, just sitting there.

Because the frog gradually adjusted to the increasing water temperature, he didn't even move. He could've jumped out of the water at any time!

You are just like the frog. Each day as you're subjected to more and more stress, the internal pressure mounts, and you adjust. You become used to the heat of the moment until you can't take it anymore.

Daily life leaves you particularly susceptible to mounting pressure for a few reasons. First, the stress comes in various forms and from multiple directions. Second, certain personality traits help make stress a bigger problem than it would be otherwise. Finally, even though it's known that chronic stress is huge problem, you were never given any real tools to keep the overwhelm from happening.

If you know what you're dealing with, it's much easier to address the problem.

Psychologists identify two kinds of stress: acute and chronic. Acute stress is relatively short-lived. It's what you encounter when faced with a novel learning situation, and it is actually good for you in the sense that it allows you to remember the event and learn from it.

Chronic stress is long-lasting. This is the kind of stress that kills. It occurs when you worry all month about how you're going to pay your bills, or when you dread going to the same old job every day, or when you're bombarded by trauma as soon as you get to the job, or when this stress at work and home just continues unabated with no end in sight.

Our bodies are well-equipped to handle short bursts of acute stress. You could even call this "good" stress. This is how we rise to our best in times of pressure, or get the heck out of a dangerous situation without having to think about it. After a burst of adrenaline, our bodies return to normal, and life continues.

Chronic stress is a bit different. When we are constantly on high alert, the stress hormones adrenaline and cortisol course through our system day after day and we begin to burn out. Exasperated, we can become depressed and begin to lose focus on the joyful aspects of our lives.

The bottom line? When we push and push ourselves, something has to give! And the wear and tear caused by chronic stress affects both our mind and our body. As our bodies tire, our feelings of well-being dissolve.

As you can see, there's a lot to deal with. Just like the frog, you may not even know that you're in hot water until it's too late.

If you're reading this, however, you're right on time.

TAKEAWAY: Knowing the forms of stress can help you deal with the challenges of your days.

Lesson 4
Feeling the Effects

*Tension is who you think you should be.
Relaxation is who you are.*
~ Chinese proverb

*If your teeth are clenched and
your fists are clenched,
your lifespan is probably clenched.*
~ Adabella Radici

Stress kills. This is not sensationalism. Many studies over the past two decades and the latest research in the field of neuroscience show this to be true.

High levels of stress left unattended underlie the statistics you've heard:

- Stress is a factor in 90% of all disease, causing or exacerbating 6 of the leading causes of death.
- Workers reporting themselves as "stressed" incur healthcare costs that are 46% higher than other employees.
- Job stress costs organizations $350 billion each year in sick time, worker's compensation, attrition, and errors.

If these stats are about the general public, what kind of impact do you think stress is having on you and the organization you work for?

Stress impacts each of the body's systems in different ways.

A steady flow of adrenaline can cause gas, stomach pain, nausea, and lead to irritable bowel syndrome. It leaves your heart rate and blood pressure elevated, increasing the risk of heart disease. It can lead to mood swings, causing emotional and physical problems.

Free-flowing aldosterone kills kidney cells and promotes hypertension.

Rampant cortisol production suppresses the immune system, produces stress ulcers, and causes the skin to thin and tear easily.

The body actually overdoses from these stress hormones. In measured doses, they help you get ready for action; excessive amounts increase the risk of many harmful conditions.

Heart disease and hypertension affect the cardiovascular system. Indigestion and ulcers affect the digestive system. Seventy percent of your immune system is contained in the digestive tract, so you're more apt to feel "sick and tired" after a few days of high stress.

Overdosing on these stress hormones throws off all the glands in the endocrine system, affecting metabolism (causing weight gain), water balance, bone development, blood sugar levels, estrogen levels in women, and testosterone levels in men. When you're chronically stressed, your sex drive is dampened permanently.

Anxiety, insomnia, back pain, shortness of breath, stiff neck, and fatigue are just a few more symptoms of chronic stress. When you live with these symptoms all the time, you start to think this is just who you are. "I have a bad back." "My body is broken." You wrongly associate who you are with the symptoms of this stressful life.

The symptoms you experience are really just signposts, pointing your focus in the direction of where there's a problem that needs a solution. The only way to escape is to stop the production of the stress hormones adrenaline, aldosterone, and cortisol.

Once you see the problem, you can do something about it.

TAKEAWAY: Unhealthy stress impacts virtually every part of your body and can be fatal.

Lesson 5
Julia's Story

It's not stress that kills us,
it is our reaction to it.
  ~ Hans Selye

Many of us feel stress and get overwhelmed
not because we're taking on too much,
but because we're taking on too little
of what really strengthens us.
  ~ Marcus Buckingham

Julia is a single mom who spent years overworking, taking on more and more—at her job and at home—before finally breaking down. She was ultimately forced to take a medical leave from her job as the office manager for a private school.

Julia cared passionately about her work, felt a strong connection with the parents of the children who attended the school, and had a vested interest in the school's proper functioning because her young daughters, ages 8 and 10, studied there.

Being a mom was her life, so she made the school her life as well.

Through this emotional attachment and tireless commitment to her work, Julia was taking on more and more stress. She worked overtime without getting paid for it. Her boss was overbearing and dishonest, and prone to fits of rage when he didn't get his way.

Because she loved certain aspects of her job, she fought hard to overlook the negativity—until she couldn't anymore.

She wasn't sleeping well and had constant headaches, all from working too much. She was miserable, and her problems had been increasing over the previous 6 months. She had little time for her friends or her family.

She had lost her sense of direction and purpose.

When she realized she couldn't remember the last time she had truly laughed and played with her children and she saw she was missing out on their childhood, she knew she needed to make some drastic changes.

A self-described "Type-A" personality, Julia felt a tremendous amount of anxiety over taking leave from her job, along with the fear of not having enough money to support herself and her children. In fact, the buildup of stress led to a worldview dominated by fear.

Her friends and family compounded this fear by voicing their doubts over Julia's decision to step away from her stressful workplace. From a traditional Chinese family, Julia's parents and siblings had very conservative views on how her situation should be handled, and this only reinforced her fears. So Julia allowed herself to be stuck, until the symptoms were too severe to overlook.

Many of us feel just the way Julia did. When you're stuck in the cycle of chronic work stress that flows right into stress at home, it's hard to see other options. Chronic stress fosters a fearful and tense outlook that prevents you from seeing opportunities elsewhere.

You might know that a change is needed, but it can just seem easier to keep your head down and do what you've always been doing.

Once you see that something has to give, this is when to take action.

TAKEAWAY: The impact of work stress on your health and mindset can be significant, especially without coping mechanisms.

Lesson 6

The Type A Personality

*As long as everything is exactly the way I want it,
I'm totally flexible.*

~ Unknown

*I'm not really a control freak, but can I show you
the right way to do that?*

~ Unknown

Personality is a key component in the stress response. The compulsive, time-pressured, aggressive, and hostile person may be a "walking time bomb" waiting to explode in almost any interaction.

As if the stress at work and at home weren't enough, most of us embody personality traits that lead to the creation of more stressful thoughts. The most prevalent is being ultra Type A.

We learned a great deal about the relationship between personality and stress from the pioneering work of researchers Meyer Friedman and Ray Rosenman, the authors of *Type A Behavior and Your Heart*.

One of Friedman and Rosenman's studies compared 80 people who were characterized as Type A (competitive with free-floating hostility) with a control group of Type B people who felt no sense of time urgency and exhibited no excessive competitive drive.

The Type B individuals had much lower serum cholesterol levels than the Type A individuals. Twenty-eight percent of the Type A sample already had heart disease, which was 7 times higher than the Type B control group.

The Type A disposition leads to more stress and more stress leads to health risks.

A hallmark tendency of being Type A is the desire to control the situation. The Type A likes to think they have a handle on things, but when they get out of control, whether at work or at home, it can be challenging.

Type As are action-oriented, easily bored, and have a need for stimulation. If it's slow, they need something to do. They like the bump in adrenaline when things are jumping. Their stress levels stay a bit higher than most other people's.

They have a strong need to be needed. So many of them are the go-to person for their circle of friends or family when things in their lives go wrong. Being called on for support makes them feel good.

As a result, they have difficulty saying "No." They're always ready to give more of themselves, scheduling more activities, projects, and errands into their day than they have time for. They don't want to disappoint others.

Behaviors they exhibit because of these traits include: failure to stop and smell the roses; hurrying the speech of others; becoming unduly irritated when forced to wait in line or drive behind a car that's going too slow; explosive speech patterns or frequent use of obscenities; competitiveness; knee-jiggling or rapid finger-tapping.

These behaviors speak to a baseline feeling of being overstressed.

We live in a Type A world, where we're always trying do more things faster. And with the pace of technology only speeding up, this isn't going to change any time soon.

Psychologists used to believe that major personality makeovers were impossible. Recently, however, researchers have begun to see that, instead of being unchangingly scripted at a young age, many of our traits amount to habitual ways of responding to the world—habits that can be unlearned.

TAKEAWAY: The reflexive way we live our lives can be harmful, but we can change.

Lesson 7
What Happens at Home?

Home is where the heart is.
～ Pliny the Elder

Home is where you feel at home and are treated well.
～ Dalai Lama

As we've begun to see, chronic stress doesn't end when you hop in the car and go home. It may feel like your home life is offering a greater challenge than the job.

This can be true if you've been at your job for many years and the work feels like second nature. You could be on autopilot and not even notice the stress anymore.

When my relationship at home started showing signs that it needed to end, I started the cycle of avoidance. Instead of having the conversation that I most dreaded, I looked forward to getting to work. There, even in the midst of all the daily craziness, I could be alone or with my friends.

You need a stable and peaceful home to return to after a hard day. When your work takes a toll and your home life doesn't help get you back to a centered place, you're in trouble.

On the other hand, what happens at work can make it more difficult to connect with family, which causes unease, which creates further separation.

Not many feel like they can talk about work-related stress with family. "They wouldn't understand anyway," you think to yourself. Or you wouldn't want to burden them—this is the job that's weighing *you* down, after all. Better to keep it to yourself.

There you sit, needing connection and support from your family, but too exhausted and burnt out to do anything about it. Your kids or spouse try to say something to you, but it doesn't get through.

Another challenge arises when you don't feel supported by your loved ones. They're part of the problem, you think, not the solution.

If home is truly where the heart is, then you need to be able to allow your heart to relax and fully arrive home. Without a home to be grounded in, you feel adrift.

Without the ability to relax at home, whether because you're so stressed you can't be still or because you check out as soon as you get there, the calming effects of arriving home are lost.

Your home must help you get out of the stressful headspace.

It doesn't have to be like a monastery, either. Kids, chores, and other demands are an unavoidable part of home life. Despite this, you can create an area in the home where you can let your guard down, where you can allow for relaxation.

A friend spent a considerable amount of time turning his backyard into a sanctuary, complete with a fountain! He planted a garden, put in some trees, grass, and a hammock. His ritual after work would be to sit there for a few minutes and just be still.

You don't always think of home as an element of your de-stress strategy, but it can and should be.

TAKEAWAY: Home should be a place to recuperate from the stress of work and not exacerbate your situation.

Lesson 8
My Realization

All work and no play makes Jack a dull boy.
~ James Howell

*You will never feel truly satisfied by work
until you are satisfied by life.*
~ Heather Schuck

The tension and strain caused by chronic stress affects your relationships both on and off the job. If you're experiencing burnout at work, the distance and disconnection you feel quickly gets spread to the home. Fights are often caused by a short fuse after a rough day and then not enough fun time.

Do you feel like you have very little time for yourself? Do you give your time away to things that you'd rather not do? Do you have trouble saying "No" to people?

If you answered "Yes" to any of these questions, you may be nurturing a dysfunctional relationship with your life outside of work.

In my darkest days at work, I blamed all of my stress and tension on the job. I thought that as soon as I left the job, I'd be better. I wouldn't have to work two jobs anymore, I'd have more time to spend with my girlfriend, and I wouldn't have to deal with all of challenges at the job. This sounded great!

So I kept working on my side business and kept trudging into work most days, too. Then came a revelation.

After about two weeks of taking ten minutes for myself every day to sit and breathe, I started to notice that my relationship with my girlfriend was no longer good for either of us. We broke up.

Then I noticed that my relationship with my business partner was making life more difficult rather than improving it. I didn't know this until after I broke up with my girlfriend. I had given all of my free time to the business project because, as long as I had work to do, I didn't have to spend time with my girlfriend.

I had been blindly devoted to a failing business venture because it helped me escape my relationship! When you're not clear about how your relationships outside of work are helping or hurting you, you may fall into traps of self-deception like I did.

After making the break with my girlfriend and my business partner—both things that were not helping my stress levels—my relationship with my work improved dramatically. I became more present with customers. I was nicer to coworkers. I started having fun again.

It took courage, though, to bust out of the old relationships. Even if you're uncomfortable with where you are, there's familiarity in that discomfort. You choose the familiar discomfort over the mystery of the unknown because at least you can count on what you know.

Chronic stress causes you to see the world through the lens of lack and limitation. Instead of seeing what's possible if you were to break free from the old way, you just stay where you are, stuck.

Evaluating the relationships you have outside of work is just as important, and perhaps more important, than evaluating your relationship to work. And by relationships outside of work, this doesn't only mean to people. How are your hobbies? How is your fun level? What about your downtime, or your relationship to being a parent, child, sibling, or friend?

Your relationships and the way you feel about them are telling you something valuable about where you're at.

> **TAKEAWAY:** Running away from aspects of your life outside work contributes to your stress, making work more difficult.

Part 2

Making the Mental Shift

Lesson 9
The Paradigm Shift

*Good health and good sense are two of
life's greatest blessings.*
~ Publilius Syrus

*The people who get on in this world are the people
who get up and look for the circumstances they
want, and, if they can't find them, make them.*
~ George Bernard Shaw

You know that stress, generally speaking, is bad. You feel it. You know that it hurts your heart, strains your mind, and makes you grumpy. Who likes being on edge all the time?

This is just like the smoker who wants to quit, knows the dangers of smoking, feels bad every time he or she lights up, but simply doesn't quit. Knowing the dangers isn't a sufficient motivator for change. You need to look at things in a different way.

When you look at things more deeply, you see that your personal approach to the stressful aspects of your life are based on your paradigms—made up of your beliefs, values, and personal convictions.

Like a broken compass, if your paradigms guide you in one direction, yet you think you're walking in another, you may end up lost.

For example, people stuck on self-pity may blame the way they were raised; many alcohol abusers are quick to blame their spouses or managers; many television addicts rationalize that they're relaxing when they're really procrastinating; people with heart disease might blame genes when diet or lifestyle is the real culprit. These are paradigms, ways of being, that promote broken-compass living.

As you know, personal paradigms are hard to change. But they do change when you are faced with situations that offer a different perspective.

The following radio conversation between a U.S. naval ship and Canadian authorities off the coast of Newfoundland illustrates how a different perspective can offer a paradigm-shifting experience that causes immediate change.

Communication: Please divert your course 15 degrees to the north to avoid a collision.

Response: Recommend you divert *your* course 15 degrees to the south to avoid a collision.

Communication: This is a Captain of a U.S. Navy ship. I say again, divert *your* course.

Response: No, I say again, you divert *your* course.

Communication: THIS IS THE AIRCRAFT CARRIER U.S.S. MISSOURI. WE ARE A LARGE WARSHIP OF THE U.S. NAVY. DIVERT YOUR COURSE NOW!

Response: This is a lighthouse. Your call.

The captain had to change his perspective, shift his paradigm. A paradigm shift results from finding a more accurate compass or a more accurate and relevant road map to arrange the beliefs and expectations you hold to select and filter the information you receive.

What beliefs and expectations define your paradigm of being Type A, working too hard, and not prioritizing your downtime?

If these beliefs and expectations lead to thoughts that don't help you get out of the stressed mindset, you may be ready for a shift! You can shift your paradigm with inspiration, practice, and dedication.

TAKEAWAY: Identify your current paradigm to find out if it's causing you stress.

Lesson 10
Your Beliefs Define Your Perspective

All that we are is the result of what we have thought.
~ Buddha

*It's not who you are that holds you back,
it's who you think you're not.*
~ Unknown

In order to shift your paradigm and put new habits in place, you need to increase your awareness of your current thoughts and practices. If you aren't aware of the thoughts and practices that got you to where you are right now, the chances of making necessary changes are slim.

A critical part of your journey is to prepare yourself well to be able to make the changes. This section of the book is your preparation to change.

You may have tried to change your situation without changing the underlying beliefs you're hanging on to. Isn't it funny that sometimes you change your circumstances but the stress seems to follow you?

Stress frequently arises from the tension between what you believe and what you actually do. Stress comes from the tension between what your parents, friends, and community influenced you to believe and what you actually believe for yourself as an adult. Stress frequently arises when you want a different life but don't believe it's possible.

Lacking the belief that something is possible means it's not possible. If you don't believe you can dramatically reduce your stress, you won't.

Consider the following simple patterns:

Goal: I'm going to lose weight.
Belief: I can't lose weight. I've never succeeded at anything.
Belief: I've tried before and it never worked.
Belief: I don't deserve to be healthy and happy because people always told me I'm no good.

Goal: I'm going to be financially secure.
Belief: My parents told me money is the root of all evil, so it's bad to have it.
Belief: I don't know how to make a lot of money, so I can't have it.
Belief: I can't imagine myself with a lot of money. That would mean I'm successful and I've never been successful at anything.

Excess weight and financial difficulties are two major sources of stress. You may want to do something about them, but you're set up for failure—and you don't even know it. That's because your underlying beliefs didn't change at all.

In order to have a paradigm shift—to do things differently—you have to change what you believe about the things you see. In turn, this will allow you to change your thoughts and behaviors that aren't serving you well.

How many times have you given up on something when it got difficult? How many times have you given up on something because you just didn't believe you could do it?

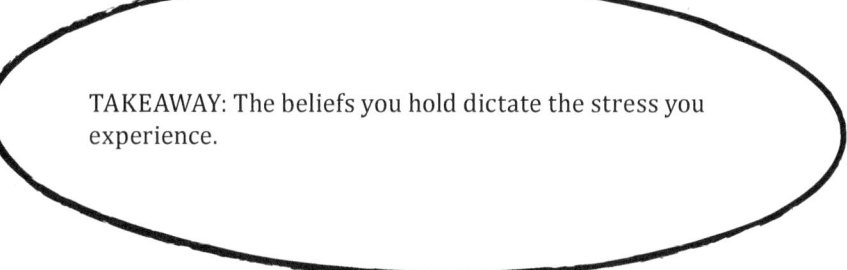

TAKEAWAY: The beliefs you hold dictate the stress you experience.

Lesson 11
The Gap between Belief and Reality

Things are not always as they seem;
the first appearance deceives many.
~ Phaedrus

To change ourselves effectively,
we first have to change our perceptions.
~ Stephen R. Covey

Of the stressors at your job, daily hassles create the most frustration: the never-ending task list, the hundreds of emails, the challenging coworkers, workplace policies and politics.

I used to be a 911 operator at the LAPD. Did you know that 70% of all calls to the 911 dispatch center in Los Angeles are non-emergencies? That means that over 2 million calls are placed each year by people reporting their daily hassles.

I remember, at first, being slightly amused by the things people called 911 for: loud parties, neighbor disputes, "my 8-year-old won't obey the house rules." After a year or two, my amusement turned to frustration.

What happened?

When I signed on for the job, I *believed* that callers would be courteous, that they would listen, and that they would know not to use 911 to report non-emergencies. I *believed* people were rational and polite. I *believed* I was working for the greater good and I would have a big impact on the community.

I never updated my beliefs or my expectations from before I started the job. For years, I rationalized my bad attitude. "The rules suck, the callers are dumb, and the supervisors are power mongers," I thought to myself as I continued to vent my frustration on the world around me.

The gap between my totally unfounded beliefs and naïve expectations on the one hand and the reality that I experienced in the communication center on the other hand created a massive amount of stress over time. In fact, this is one of the key definitions of stress. When things don't look the way you think they should, you experience stress.

And often you simply check out. You overeat, smoke, binge on TV, put in minimal effort at work, have a lousy attitude, and a whole bunch of other things to cope with your stress.

The bigger the gap between your expectations and reality, the greater the stress.

I had to face facts. Seventy percent of all calls are non-emergency. In a city like Los Angeles, where I worked, nearly 3 million calls come through the communication center each year. I had to change my beliefs. I had to reduce the gap between my expectations and reality.

You can either *let yourself* be frustrated by the way things are or you can try something else.

This isn't to say that you shouldn't expect a level of common decency and respect from your coworkers and colleagues or that you should just be OK with everything. But, there are beliefs you're hanging on to that help create your stress and undermine your own best interests.

Identify a few of your beliefs and expectations that need updating right now. What past thoughts are you holding on to, feeling justified in being angry about, when it might be better to just let them go?

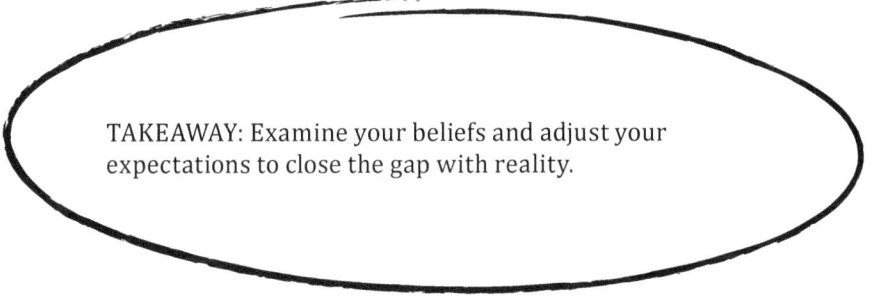

TAKEAWAY: Examine your beliefs and adjust your expectations to close the gap with reality.

Lesson 12
Values: Knowing What's Important

*When your values are clear to you,
making decisions becomes easier.*
~ Roy E. Disney

*The value of life is not in the length of days,
but in the use we make of them; one may
live long yet very little.*
~ Michel de Montaigne

When you stop to consider what you believe, you'll start to express your beliefs in the form of values. If you believe that you or others should not lie, cheat, or steal, one of your values might be expressed as integrity.

You determined your values by what you chose to believe. Of course, many of your beliefs and values came from the environment you grew up in and the way your family, friends, and community influenced you.

Your beliefs and your values have guided the thoughts you've had and the actions you've taken.

BELIEFS —> VALUES —> THOUGHTS —> ACTIONS

Part of your stress comes from standing by inherited beliefs and values that you may not believe anymore. Another source of stress is standing by beliefs and values that other people expect you to have. You try to satisfy both your needs and their needs, and that doesn't always work.

An effective way to identify your values is to look at what you believe is important for your life. Beyond the physical requirements of food, shelter, and community, what must you have in your life in order to be fulfilled? Values could be: authenticity, integrity, love, intimacy, commitment, health, prosperity, excellence, or many other things.

Take some time now to brainstorm a list of the ten values that are important you.

Now, select your top three in order of importance to you.

1.
2.
3.

To the right of these, score your sense of satisfaction—the degree to which you are honoring each value—using a scale of 0 to 10 where 0 means you're not honoring that value and 10 means you're living the values you proclaim to have.

This exercise can be particularly revealing if you find that you are not honoring the values that are highest on your list. Rankings below 7 may indicate an area of your life where you are putting up with an intolerable situation.

Looking at the example below, you will see inconsistencies between the importance of the value and level of satisfaction rankings:

Value	Importance	Level of Satisfaction
Integrity	1	4
Freedom	2	8
Authenticity	3	5

If these were your top three, you might see that, as a result of not living with integrity, you feel a certain amount of internal tension or frustration. In other words, stress.

Not all stress is created by causes that we're immediately aware of; sometimes it takes a little self-reflection to understand what's going on. Once you've uncovered the underlying reason, you can make a shift.

> TAKEAWAY: Your values, and how you live them, play a large role in the stress you allow in your life.

Lesson 13
Priorities: Doing What's Important

Action expresses priorities.
~ Mahatma Gandhi

It is not enough to be busy, so are the ants.
The question is, 'What are we busy about?'
~ Henry David Thoreau

What do you believe, and what values are important to you?

If you don't know, it will be pretty difficult, if not impossible, to decide what your priorities should be.

One of the tricks to reducing stress is understanding clearly what's important to you and then making those things your priorities. As Stephen Covey, author of *The 7 Habits of Highly Effective People*, says, "Put first things first."

You can't do that if you don't know what's supposed to be first.

When you figure out your priorities based on your beliefs and values, you also determine what is *not* worth pursuing. If you don't know your priorities, you'll end up chasing the wrong things or too many things. This creates stress.

One thing should be clear: you will always have priorities.

The question is will they be priorities that you consciously choose or will they just be things that happen to you while you're locked down in your stress?

So often you declare your priorities and yet your actions don't reflect your words. You say your health is important, but your diet consists of fast food.

You say your family is important, but you never spend time with them. You say financial security is important, but you don't save any money.

By the way, there's really no need to declare your priorities to anyone else; you will show others your priorities by what you do.

For example, if you say you're going to exercise and lose weight, but instead you spend hours in front of the television and eat three pizzas a week, watching television and eating pizza are, in reality, your priorities. And guess what? This creates stress.

Remember the expectation gap from Lesson 11? Part of that gap is created by not knowing or living your priorities.

As with belief and values, establishing your priorities is not an exercise in a vacuum to be done for its own sake. It's a necessary part of moving forward to reduce stress, avoid burnout, and get what you want.

When you know what your priorities are, based on your beliefs and values, it's easier to manage your time and say "No" to people. It's easier to resist the gossiping, blaming, and criticizing that contribute to your stress. It's easier to focus on what needs to get done. It reduces stress.

By the way, you may be tempted to blow right past the exercises in this book and not give too much thought to your beliefs, values, and priorities. I get it. But doing the exercises was exactly how I was able to make my shift without quitting my job.

This trio of beliefs, values, and priorities forms one of the most important keys in making the transition to relaxation.

TAKEAWAY: Priorities based on beliefs and values will guide your actions.

Lesson 14
Looking Deeper

*90% of an iceberg is beneath the water's surface.
It's what's below that will sink your ship.*
　～ U.S. Coast Guard

*Keep looking below surface appearances.
Don't shrink from doing so
just because you might not like what you find.*
　～ Colin Powell

Stressors at work and home are a factor in bringing you into the chronically stressed zone, but they aren't the cause of stressful feelings. In fact, they are a much smaller factor than you might imagine. As we've discussed, stress is largely created by your thoughts and perceptions. These thoughts and perceptions arise from your beliefs, which are connected to your deeper ways of seeing the world.

When you blame only the external circumstances for how stressed you feel, playing the victim to things out of your control, you miss a whole world of information. Looking below the surface at the more subtle dimensions of your stress-prone personality helps you see areas where you can shore up your defenses.

Your Type A-ness is only part of the story. Your baseline level of anxiety, feelings of self-esteem, and locus of control also bear weight on the situation. Let's have a look.

Anxiety is that itchy feeling that forces you to be jumpy, never sit still, and twitch your leg or tap your pen. Enduring years of stress in a lousy job or an unhealthy relationship can ratchet up your anxiety level, making it hard to sleep.

With anxiety, you don't quite feel comfortable in your own skin. You're overly sensitive, always keyed up. Even when you want to relax, you can't. Anxiety is most often driven by being overly conscious of the criticisms and judgment of others. It can also be spurred on by unrealistic drives to be perfect. Anxiety is a result of the gap between belief or expectations and reality.

Self-esteem is closely related to anxiety. If you have a poor self-image and low self-esteem, you perceive a larger number of life situations as potentially threatening (psychologically and physically). Viewing the world as hostile, you get anxious and more guarded.

Self-esteem is directly related to expectations for success. Those with high self-esteem are more likely to feel that they will succeed and will take greater risks. Low self-esteem causes you to be more susceptible to external influences and depend on others for approval.

Some of us believe we are in control and masters of our own destiny. Others see life as being determined by the randomness of external events, believing that what happens in life is due to chance or circumstance.

If you believe that life is controlled by outside forces, you have an external locus of control. If you believe that life's directions can be controlled by your own actions, you have an internal locus of control.

Those with an external locus of control, believing they can't control life events, are shown to be less satisfied with their jobs, call in sick more frequently, and are less engaged at work. They are more stressed because they perceive that they have little ability to affect outcomes.

Identifying where you are in these areas will help you more clearly see the underlying causes of your stress. Later on, we'll discuss specific ways to develop greater self-esteem, lower anxiety, and shift to a more internal locus of control.

TAKEAWAY: Look deeper inside yourself to understand the causes of your anxiety.

Lesson 15
E + R = O

*Between stimulus and response there is a space.
In that space is our power to choose our response.
In our response lies our growth and our freedom.*
~ Viktor Frankl

*The great majority of emotional distress
we experience results from how we think about
ourselves and our circumstances, rather than the
circumstances themselves.*
~ Thom Rutledge

Burnout is caused by long-term stress driven by a large gap between your expectations and realities. This often creates the illusion that you don't have a choice anymore.

You've been making so many judgments from a place of being totally stressed out that you think it's either normal or out of your control.

When you're clear about your beliefs, values, priorities, and whether you're driven by an internal or external locus of control, you'll have a much better idea how to respond to things that happen around you.

Whether you realize it or not, you get to choose how you respond to each and every event that happens.

Events themselves are value neutral. They just "are." It's the way you see events that gives them their meaning. Much of your stress comes from *your judgment* of events that happen. Much of your stress is driven by what you choose to believe.

And then this stress strongly influences the way you see events and the way you react to them. See how this becomes a never-ending loop?

The basic equation to summarize this is $E + R = O$, where E is an Event that occurs, R is your Response to the Event, and O is the Outcome you are getting in your life. What Outcomes are you getting? Are you getting the Outcomes you want? Are you living the life you want?

If you want to change the Outcomes, you have to change your Responses.

There is no way around that. Successful people get what they want because they pay close attention to their Responses, because they know their Responses drive their Outcomes.

While there may be several or numerous factors involved, your Response to the Event may be the only thing in your control, the only thing you can change. You can't change the Event after it happens. You can't change other people.

But, you can change the way you look at the Event and you can change your Response. That's it.

Increasing your awareness helps expand the set of responses you have in your toolkit and zap your stress. (See Dr. Joe Serio's book, *Overcoming Fear: 50 Lessons on Being Bold and Living the Dream* for his 7-Step Action Plan for Managing Fear.)

In the quote above, Viktor Frankl essentially is saying you should draw out your Response time to Events.

When you draw out your Response time, you can formulate a more thoughtful Response rather than reacting instantaneously. You can then improve your Responses.

When you improve your Responses, you improve your Outcomes, and you change your life.

TAKEAWAY: You can change your Outcomes in life by changing your Responses to the Events around you.

Lesson 16
Fight or Flight...or the Third Way

Adopting the right attitude can convert a negative stress into a positive one.
~ Hans Selye

Slow down and everything you are chasing will come around and catch you.
~ John De Paola

Imagine it's 10,000 B.C. and you're leading your tribe through treacherous terrain, constantly scanning the horizon for threats, all senses alert to the possibility of danger.

Suddenly, a saber-toothed cat leaps from behind a rock and takes chase.

In an instant, your pituitary gland signals the adrenal glands to flood your bloodstream with stress hormones, including adrenaline, aldosterone, and cortisol.

Your heart rate increases, you hyperventilate, more oxygen flows throughout your body, and your senses heighten further as blood is directed away from digestion and other non-essential functions.

Your immune system is suppressed to free up resources.

You can run faster, perform with more strength, think more quickly, respond through instinct, and feel less pain—all because of this natural response to imminent danger.

Fight or flight.

After you have successfully fought or fled the threat and found a place to relax, your body's systems return to normal. The levels of adrenaline and cortisol in your bloodstream decrease, causing your heart rate to lower, blood pressure to drop, and all other functions of the body to come back online.

At the heart of your issue with stress and burnout is your inability to turn off your fight-or-flight response mechanism. The imbalance in your beliefs, values, priorities, reactions to events, and a lot of other factors keeps you constantly pumping stress hormones. You're in constant fight-or-flight mode.

Being in constant fight-or-flight mode impacts your communication, focus, nutrition, and health. It undermines your performance and productivity. You get less sleep, drink more caffeine, and generally feel rundown.

Furthermore, without unplugging from the continual onslaught of stress hormones, your body eventually breaks down. Exactly where your blowout occurs depends on your body, but, since so many of your natural systems are affected by chronic stress, there are ample chances for burnout.

Beating the burnout means reducing stress so it doesn't become chronic and coming to the realization that there is a third way other than fight or flight. That's the key: finding that third way to handle situations.

The third way is the relaxation response. It presents itself as an alternative when stress—fight or flight—is not the best response.

After I wrap up the transition section, I'll give you numerous ways to activate the relaxation response and start getting on the road to health and wellness.

> TAKEAWAY: Fight or flight can be important to your well-being, but not if it's turned on all the time.

Lesson 17

Choose the Story of Your Life Wisely

Everyone is necessarily the hero of his own life story.
> ~ John Barth

*Believe in yourself. Have faith in your abilities.
Without a humble but reasonable
confidence in your abilities,
you cannot be successful or happy.*
> ~ Norman Vincent Peale

What is the story you choose to tell yourself about your life?

Is it one of hardship and struggle or one of accomplishment and joy?

Do you like where you are or are you waiting for some future date to be happy?

For years, the story I told myself about my life was one of hardship and struggle. My parents didn't give me enough attention growing up. Nothing I did was ever good enough. I could never get a lucky break. Supervisors at work were always gunning for me.

I was always in a hurry to get somewhere else, because, whatever was happening, *now* was no fun. And so I would rush around, tense and anxious, honking at anyone who got in my way (literally and figuratively).

This way of approaching the world—through my story of constant struggle—caused regular disappointment. Nothing ever measured up to the way I thought things should look. There was a never-ending sense of urgency about my days. I was fast approaching burnout.

Disappointment, time urgency, and burnout are some of the stress warning signs that arise from the story that you tell yourself. I'll list more in the next lesson.

You live with your symptoms for so long that you overly identify with them, believing that you *are* your symptoms.

You pride yourself on your perfectionism, not seeing how it erodes your happiness and increases the pressure you put on yourself and the world around you. You feel satisfaction as you vent your anger and hostility, hoping to control the uncontrollable.

"I'm just an angry person," you declare. Or, "My perfectionism makes me better at my job," you think.

Instead of seeing anger and perfectionism for what they really are—learned behaviors—you take them on as unchangeable aspects of who you are.

But, you can unlearn some of your old habits, reframe your self-concept, and take control of a more desired behavior.

When I began slowing down, taking more time for myself, reflecting on my life, and realizing I had a choice about which story I could tell, beautiful things began to happen.

I saw that my life has been a series of amazing adventures aided by a cast of loving and supportive friends. I realized that my parents did the very best they could. Even the challenges I've met along the way, while sometimes difficult, have provided the influence I needed to grow and expand.

Bring to mind a challenge you faced in the past. What was something good that came out of meeting that challenge? Focusing on the positive brings strength and turns future challenges into opportunities for growth.

TAKEAWAY: The way you tell your story matters and affects how you are now as you move into the future.

Lesson 18
The Warning Signs

*In order to go on living, one must try to escape
the death involved in perfectionism.*
~ Hannah Arendt

*Anger is an acid that can do more harm to the vessel
in which it stored than
to anything on which it is poured.*
~ Mark Twain

Living through a personal story of hardship and struggle takes its toll. This toll impacts you in the form of the seven stress warning signs developed by Dr. Jim Petersen. Knowing what they are and how they affect you shows you where and what to change.

The Seven Stress Warning Signs

1. **Anger** is the main sign that you're under stress. It's a reaction designed with the intent to control others and their behavior. When you don't get what you want, expect, or demand, you vent anger in frustration.

2. **Perfectionism** is not the same as excellence or doing things very well. It's often based on the belief that unless you are perfect, you are not OK. It's also an intense competition with yourself—a need to be something that is not possible at the moment. It is a drive to make sure that everything has its place, that you are completely organized, completely smart, completely worthy. Perfectionism is deeply based in a fear of failure and a fear of losing the approval or love of others.

3. **Time urgency** is a huge factor in our fast-paced, technology-driven culture. It's often called time sickness, where you are married to the clock, trying to do too many things at once. By doing things too fast or all at once, you reduce your effectiveness, lower the quality of your work, and waste your time.

4. **Disappointment** has been shown to have the highest correlation with negative stress effects. It is the result of expectations that are not being met by the world. These expectations or hopes are either too high or inappropriate for the person or situation. When you carry disappointment around with you for prolonged periods of time, it produces chronic stress.

5. **Burnout** is one of the primary indicators of prolonged exposure to stress. Burnout is an emotional state that predominates a person's life. People who are experiencing burnout move more slowly than usual, do not laugh at themselves, and are fearful.

6. **Underachievement** is directly related to your interpretation of how well you are doing; feelings of underachievement are often reflected in excessively high personal standards. You may actually be doing many things; however, you may not feel or think you are achieving much. Whereas disappointment is largely related to others not meeting your expectations, underachievement is disappointment with yourself.

7. **Tension** is the result of carrying physical and emotional stress around on a daily basis. Tension manifests as headaches, migraines, aches, and pains and can often mean you're not taking the time to slow down and relax. Aside from the physical pain, tension can result in poor decision making, reduced energy, increased errors, and difficulty concentrating.

Look at the stress warning signs and compare them to your life.

Do you see yourself in any of them? Which one(s)?

How do the warning signs affect the Responses you give to Events that happen in your life?

TAKEAWAY: Determine how the seven stress warning signs are impacting your life to see the opportunity for change.

Lesson 19
Make Your Relationships Work for You

Tell your boss what you really think about him, and the truth shall set you free, from your job.
~ Unknown

If you're in a relationship and you want it to work, you have to be a little selfless sometimes.
~ Montel Williams

You wake up one morning, still angry about the fight you had with your husband the night before. He's already up making breakfast, which means, thankfully, you have some time alone to shower and get ready for the day. In the shower, you begin thinking about work, dreading having to work another day at your company.

Both of these important relationships are now creating tension. You feel anger and frustration with your husband and dread about work. Already this is feeling like a tough day, and it's barely started!

Your entire outlook on life comes down to how good you feel about your relationships: the relationships with people, like with your spouse, kids, friends, and coworkers, as well as the more subtle relationships that you may not even regard as relationships, like with the office technology, your car, or your morning commute.

Yes, you have a relationship with your car. Maybe you have a name for her/him. You might pamper your car, treat it like your baby. Relationships are not just with people.

Over the course of the day, you are in constant interaction with your various relationships. When most of your relationships are strained and colored with difficulty, what does that do to your feelings of effectiveness, to your level of happiness and hope?

When experiencing your relationships through the lens of any of the seven stress warning signs, things can quickly move from bad to worse.

You've been there, having a difficult conversation with someone who won't take "No" for an answer. Even if it's said politely. You think of the choice words you'd *like* to say, but won't since you'd also like to keep your job.

So, you have to pay attention to how you're feeling about these relationships and address certain feelings before they run away from you.

Looking at your relationship with the various elements of your job, what do you see? Are you looking through the lens of any of the stress warning signs: anger, disappointment, time urgency, burnout, perfectionism, underachievement, or tension?

The best way to begin this self-inquiry is to start with a general ranking of how you feel about work.

Take out a blank piece of paper. Write "overall satisfaction" somewhere on the paper. On a scale of 1 to 10, 1 being the least and 10 being the most, rate your level of satisfaction with your job.

From here, write down some of the specific elements of your job that go into this "overall" category. Coworkers, supervision, workload, job function, and shift hours are all possible categories to examine. Now, in the same way, rank these specific categories on the 1-to-10 scale.

Looking at the lower numbers, see if you can determine if these areas are causing you stress. Which of the stress warning signs do you see?

Untangling the specific areas of the job that cause stress allows you to see that, instead of the entire job creating stress, there may only be certain things that get to you. This makes things much more manageable.

TAKEAWAY: "Work" isn't necessarily stressful, just certain aspects of the job.

Lesson 20
Taking Charge of Your Life

*Once you replace your negative thoughts
with positive ones,
you'll start having positive results.*
~ Willie Nelson

*If you change the way you look at things,
the things you look at change.*
~ Dr. Wayne Dyer

As you realize by now, any and all personal change begins with a change in your beliefs and the way you think. This is worth repeating once more before we move forward because it's the core of everything you will encounter throughout the rest of the book.

Equally important to understand is that you can't change others; you can only influence them to make their own changes.

When you think about the things that you believe are adding stress to your life, it's easy to start blaming others.

"That supervisor's gunning for me!" you exclaim.

"I'm always being asked to do more work! Don't they know how much work I'm *already* doing?!" you gripe.

"My coworker's trying my last nerve," you mutter, defeated.

The challenge with blaming others for your stressful feeling is that there's nothing you can do about it except wait for them to change. "How long?" you ask. Who knows? That's not how personal change works.

It's your task to take 100% responsibility for the way *you* are thinking, feeling, and responding at any given moment.

Remember, E + R = O.

When I was working at the LAPD 911 Center, I had a strong attachment to the personal work I was doing *instead* of the actual dispatcher/call-taker work. In between calls or radio transmissions, I would read, play games, or do schoolwork. I was so productive that I earned a bachelor's degree, doing most of the coursework while on the job.

When I started to take a closer look at why I was so miserable, I noticed something. I was so attached to doing my personal work that when the tone sounded in my ear signaling an incoming call, I was already annoyed at the caller, *before they even said a word!* How dare they interrupt my study time!

This was an interesting discovery. So I tried an experiment.

When working the phones, especially when the lines were busy, I would put my reading and other work in the console drawer, out of sight, and just take calls. One call at a time.

I found that I was much less angry as the shift went on, and that I was more courteous to callers, because I wasn't bringing any of my displaced annoyance into each call.

For years, I had blamed the callers, blamed the busyness of the shift, blamed *anyone and anything* for the unhappiness I was feeling, when the real cause was right here, between my ears.

> TAKEAWAY: When you take 100% responsibility for your life, you unlock your personal power.

Lesson 21
Laura Makes the Transition

*If you cannot see where you are going,
ask someone who has been there before.*
~ J. Loren Norris

*Always be yourself, express yourself,
have faith in yourself;
do not go out and look for a successful personality
and duplicate it.*
~ Bruce Lee

It can be daunting to think about making your transformation out of your comfortable, yet limiting, old ways and into a life of less stress.

But, by now, you know it's possible. The choice is yours.

Here are two stories that illustrate what I've been discussing so far. The first shows the wrong way to go about it. The second is a story of victory and transformation.

Ted is a 60-year-old male, a former architect who weighs about 130-140 pounds. He jogs, is compulsive in following a strict no-fat diet, and is constantly reading books and articles on stress and health.

Ted has experienced some problems throughout his medical history. He has had three strokes, two heart attacks, and a quadruple heart bypass operation. His arteries are now just as clogged as they were several years ago, and he is awaiting an operation to relieve a 5-millimeter aneurysm in his stomach.

Ted's personality is that of a very stress-prone individual. He is vindictive, negative, skeptical, pessimistic, and critical. He lacks any sense of humor. Three wives have left him, two adult children refuse to talk to him, and he has few friends.

As we see with Ted, if the mind isn't healthy, the body can never be healthy, no matter how healthy you think you are.

The story of Laura is much more hopeful.

Laura is a 30-year-old dispatcher of 12 years, mother of 3, who had suffered from migraines and exhaustion for years. She would work her shift at the dispatch center, then go home and get right back to work caring for her three boys (four if you count her husband!).

Years of this began to run her into the ground. I could see the pain in her face and the tension in her shoulders, neck, and back. Sometimes she would seem OK while at work, but most days her response to the question, "How are you today?" was a depressed, "I'm here."

Laura was a caregiver to the world. She gave her all to her work, and then she went home and gave her all to her family. But, without giving back to herself, she was running on empty.

At one of her low points, Laura got sick. She was off work for two weeks. Back from sick leave, I asked where she had been.

"Adam, I got really sick," she said. "But something amazing happened. I asked my family to help at home, and they did! Now that I'm back at work, they're still doing their newly-assigned duties!"

I could see that she felt lighter and she looked much more relaxed.

Laura's illness caused her to look at her beliefs and expectations and question them. She stepped out of her old ways and into less stress.

TAKEAWAY: The way you think is critically important. Doing "healthy" things in a stressful way can't save you.

Part 3

Steps to Reducing Your Stress

Lesson 22
Destination Relaxation

Nothing can bring you peace but yourself.
~ Ralph Waldo Emerson

There is more to life than increasing its speed.
~ Mohandas K. Gandhi

Once you've identified the old mental programming that creates your chronically stressed life, it's time to let it go. All of it. Relaxation is the key to getting free of the old paradigm.

When I talk about relaxation, I'm not talking about going to the spa, getting a massage, or going on vacation. These can be good things for moments of relaxation, but this type of relaxation doesn't last.

A recent poll taken of 1,000 workers speaks to this. When asked, "Is vacation a cure for the work-stress blues?" 57% of respondents reported no relief from stress as a result of vacation. And that's not all. Twenty-seven percent reported *more stress* as a result of vacation!

Instead of trying to check-out but still finding signs of stress waiting for you, you can use the body's relaxation response to stop the stress for good.

In 1973, Dr. Herbert Benson, then Associate Professor of Medicine at Harvard Medical School, discovered that by using simple breathing techniques, you can elicit bodily changes that decrease heart rate, lower metabolism, decrease breathing rate, enhance well-being, and bring the body into a healthy balance.

Dr. Benson coined this body function the "relaxation response"—the converse to the stress response (fight or flight). There are four essential elements to turning on the relaxation response:

1. A quiet environment
2. An object of focus or attention
3. A passive attitude
4. A comfortable position

When used for 10-20 minutes once or twice daily, the relaxation response stops the body from producing stress hormones while calming rampant thoughts, ending fidgetiness and anxiety, and creating more space to breathe.

In time and with practice, the relaxation response helps Type A people become more Type B. Traits that exemplify "Type B-ness" include being relaxed, easygoing, seldom impatient, not easily irritated, not preoccupied with social achievement, and taking the time to enjoy.

In this Type A society with your Type A job, you might fear being more relaxed. You see everyone around you running here and there getting so much done so you feel you have to do the same—just another aspect of keeping up with the Joneses. But at what cost?

You're even told or shown that if you're not stressed about the things in your life, you don't care enough.

Think about a recent argument you had with your spouse. In that moment where you finally surrender your point, you lower your voice, relax your shoulders, and disengage from battle, your spouse says, "Oh, I see, you just don't care!" Because you no longer seemed stressed about what's going on, it's interpreted as detachment, complacency, or lack of interest.

With the relaxation response, you can meet your daily experiences in the moment, without the tension and aggression of the stress response of fight or flight. All it takes is a little practice.

TAKEAWAY: The relaxation response is the gateway to being more Type B.

Lesson 23
Relaxation Techniques

For fast-acting relief, try slowing down.
~ Lily Tomlin

*Sometimes the most productive thing
you can do is relax.*
~ Mark Black

Now that you've gone through your transition and understand how the mind has to change in order to approach relaxation, let's get right into the easiest, most effective way to reduce stress. Let's turn on Dr. Benson's relaxation response.

The beauty of this practice is that you can use it at your desk, in the car, and at home to quickly let go of what's bothering you.

Mindfulness

Mindfulness, put simply, is noticing. Try it now. Notice your body posture. Are you slouching? Do you feel any tension anywhere? Notice how this book feels in your hands. Notice any thoughts, feelings, or other body sensations.

Now notice sounds. You can hear sounds close to you and then sounds a bit further away. As you tune into a sound, are there any thoughts associated with this sound? What do you see?

The point of mindfulness is to come into contact with as many of the five senses at once without holding on to anything. As sensations arise, notice how they fall away. Without grasping or clinging, you are able to let things pass—good thoughts *and* more challenging thoughts or sensations—much more easily.

Deep Breathing

When you're stressed, you breathe in tight little breaths in your upper chest. This causes tremendous upper body tension, your shoulders to be drawn up toward your ears, and stagnation of energy in the body.

Consciously taking a few breaths deep into the lower belly helps to release this upper body tension, oxygenate the blood, and stimulate the flow of energy throughout the muscles.

Try it now. Imagine a point in the lower belly, a bit below your navel towards the back of the body, and draw the breath into this point. You'll know you're doing it right when your abdomen inflates with this in-breath, and deflates with the out-breath.

Progressive Relaxation

When you're mindful of your tension and can breathe deeply into your lower belly, you're ready to use the mind to release the tension you've been holding on to. Like setting down a bag of rocks you didn't know you were carrying, you can literally unravel the tension in your muscles just by allowing for it.

Sit in a comfortable position. Do a quick scan of your body. Where are you tense? Do you notice pain, tightness, numbness, or density somewhere?

Let your awareness rest on an area of tension. Now, on the in-breath, draw the breath into this area of tension, intensifying the feeling a bit. Then on the out-breath, completely relax. Imagine the tension melting down out of your body and into the earth. As you let go of one layer of tension, see if you can let go of another. And another.

Connecting the mind with the body (through any of the five senses) brings your focus into the present moment. This is a moment between thoughts. It is here where you can relax.

TAKEAWAY: Relaxing the body relaxes the mind, instantly creating the opportunity for more space.

Lesson 24
Slow Yourself Down

*Nature does not hurry,
yet everything is accomplished.*
~ Lao Tzu

*You're only here for a short visit.
Don't hurry, don't worry.
And be sure to smell the flowers along the way.*
~ Walter Hagen

More and more people are finding the courage to slow down. They're tired of the constant running. They're intentionally scheduling less. They're saying "No" more often. They're turning off their cell phones on the weekend and asking their kids to do the same.

This is a huge step toward relaxation.

The mind, conditioned by the stress hormones adrenaline, noradrenaline, and cortisol, sees the world through the lens of lack and limitation. When you fear for your survival, which is how the body responds every time you get stressed, you are reflexively defensive and hurried. Of course you're hurried and distracted—your body and mind thinks you're under constant attack!

Since you've spent so much of your life rushing around trying to get things done, time urgency is a major factor for many. You pride yourself on being swift and like others to see that you care enough to hustle.

Hustling because you need to be somewhere in a short amount of time is one thing, but being in a hurry *all the time* and growing impatient with others because they're going *so dang slow* is something else altogether.

I was guilty of this for years. My need to rush, and rush others, manifested as rude shortness with callers, road rage (and honkaholism), and a condescending tone with people. There seemingly was no time for courtesy—I'm in a hurry!

This changed when I stopped giving all my time away and started doing things that I genuinely enjoyed. When you like what you're doing, why rush?

This leads to more time and space to enjoy life. But it takes a break from the norm to make it happen.

I notice that many who really care about their work are born caregivers. They take care of everyone in their circle. At the 911 center, it was the same. I was always amazed at how much money was raised at the dispatch center for families in need during difficult times.

This caregiving nature is beautiful…unless it prevents you from replenishing your own health and well-being. On the other side of the coin, many of my dispatcher friends wish they could say "No" more often and take better care of themselves.

Why can't you? For whatever reason, there's a fear of being seen as selfish. So you keep agreeing to things you'd rather not do and then rushing around to get it all crammed into a day. With kids and a merciless commute, the days easily blur together. (See Dr. Joe Serio's book, *Time Management: 50 Lessons on Finding Time for What's Important*.)

Slowing down enough to see a difference doesn't require you to stop doing the things that matter to you. The commitment to slowing down is just about being more selective, in the interest of being able to give more of yourself to what you *do* choose to take on, instead of blindly saying "Yes" to everything.

If given the choice, what would you say "No" to this week? How would you say "Yes" to yourself?

TAKEAWAY: Slowing down is a powerful way to de-stress and be more connected to things that matter most.

Lesson 25
No More Avoidance

I am always doing what I cannot do yet, in order to learn how to do it.
~ Vincent Van Gogh

So many people prefer to live in drama because it's comfortable. It's like someone staying in a bad marriage or relationship— it's actually easier to stay because they know what to expect every day, versus leaving and not knowing what to expect.
~ Ellen DeGeneres

By this point, you should have a sense of where you are and where you'd like to go in relation to your feelings of stress and burnout. You may even know exactly what needs to be done. So what's keeping you from taking the next step?

Uncertainty. Fear. Apprehension. Avoidance.

At one of my speaking engagements someone from the audience came up to me afterwards and said, "You were speaking right to me! I've been dealing with a toxic relationship at home for a long time now, and I know what I have to do, but I keep delaying. I wish my partner would take action so I didn't have to make the move."

For months she had been putting up with miserable circumstances, delaying the inevitable, and now, finally, she was coming to the realization that, if *anything* was going to happen, she was going to be the one to do it. But she still hadn't done it.

You've been here. Staring opportunity in the face, yet succumbing to procrastination and avoidance.

What are your excuses for not taking action today?

The audience member didn't want to start looking for a new place to live. She didn't want to hurt her soon-to-be-ex's feelings. She didn't really feel like upsetting the seeming comfort of her living situation even though it was less than inspiring. She didn't want to tear off the Band-Aid quickly—it stings!

A powerful technique for overcoming avoidance is visualization. The following three-step visualization technique has been used by professional athletes around the world.

1. Think about your task as already being complete. Imagine what it would look like, feel like, and sound like. The more senses you can use, the more powerful your visualization will be. What benefits will come from accomplishing this task? How relieved will you feel once it is over?
2. Intensify the pleasant feelings that you've associated with the completion of your task. Make your images bigger and brighter. Make the feelings more intense, the sounds louder, richer, and more powerful. The idea is to create an exaggerated version of reality, one that excites and energizes you.
3. Now, stop what you are doing and start your task immediately. It's very important to take some form of action right away because the motivational energy you've generated with this exercise will fade.

This can be used in almost any situation where you're feeling pulled into the avoidance trap. Want to exercise more? Prepare for an interview? Have that challenging conversation? Imagine it done!

Then, do it. Some of us wait for tomorrow, but tomorrow never comes—the time is always now.

TAKEAWAY: Avoidance is fear in disguise. Taking action is the surest way to banish any fear.

Lesson 26
Cultivating Resilience

Man never made any material as resilient as the human spirit.
~ Bern William

Resilient people immediately look at the problem and say, "What's the solution to that? What is this trying to teach me?"
~ Jack Canfield

Why do some people thrive in the midst of daily challenges while others get taken out? Why can some people tolerate a tremendous amount of stress and others get sick?

Resilience.

Resilience is the ability to bounce back in the face of hardship and adversity, and perform your best on a consistent basis. Like a stress ball that returns to its original shape after being squeezed, the resilient recover more quickly than others when life's pressures mount. While we may have different levels of resilience to begin with based on heredity or psychological disposition, we can increase our resiliency over time.

Ten psychological and social factors have been identified as making a person more resilient:
1. Facing fear
2. Having a moral compass
3. Drawing on faith
4. Using social support

5. Having good role models
6. Being physically fit
7. Making sure your brain is challenged
8. Having cognitive and emotional flexibility
9. Having meaning, purpose, and growth in life
10. Being optimistic

Used together, these factors have a powerful effect in the face of major trauma and in the day-to-day stresses of life as well.

There are four strategies for cultivating resilience in the face of daily stressors:

1. **Change your stressors.** Once you've experienced a stressor, it can't be reversed or prevented, but you can make adjustments so that future events don't cause stress. For example, learning de-stress techniques can help make you more clear and focused.

2. **Remove yourself from your stressors.** After facing a difficult situation, you can take a few minutes for yourself to help release some pressure. You have to be careful not to fall into an avoidance trap, though, which can turn into passive-aggressive behavior.

3. **Change your thinking.** This is the most powerful tool you have for increasing resilience. Truly, how you feel is a result of what you are thinking. In a later lesson, you'll learn nine thinking styles that most often lead to high stress levels. (Remember: E + R = O)

4. **Reduce the effects of stress.** Your breathing practice, taking time for yourself, having fun, and balancing your work with a hefty dose of play are all great ways to reduce the effects of stress and increase resilience. I'll cover ways to reduce the effects of stress in more detail later.

Each of these strategies helps relax the stress response. As you become more resilient, you continually see other ways of choosing less stress.

TAKEAWAY: Becoming more resilient is critical in preventing stress from taking over.

Lesson 27
What You Focus On Expands

*The worst times can be the best
if you think with positive energy.*
~ Domenico Dolce

*The people who live in a golden age usually
go around complaining how yellow everything looks.*
~ Randall Jarrell

Working while stressed out all day can leave a mark. When you're annoyed and frustrated, complaining come naturally. The talk around the water cooler begins to reflect this discontent as well. When you participate in the discussion, you get just as fired up as those involved, dragging yourself through someone else's mud. Misery loves company, doesn't it?

In these moments there is a great opportunity to choose. After all, if *you* don't protect your positivity, no one else will.

The field of positive psychology has shown us a lot about what's possible when people orient their lives around positive things. Positive psychology is the scientific study of what makes life most worth living. Instead of a focus on what's wrong, as in traditional psychology, positive psychology teaches that what's good in life is not simply the absence of what's problematic. You can find things to be grateful for or happy about regardless of your life circumstances.

Studies in positive psychology have given new cause to believe in the power of positivity. A few of the findings:

- Happiness is a cause of good things in life. People who are satisfied with life eventually have even more reason to be satisfied, because happiness leads to desirable outcomes at school and work, fulfilling social relationships, and even good health and long life.

- Happiness, strength of character, and good social relationships are buffers against the damaging effects of disappointments and setbacks.

- Good days have common features: feeling autonomous, competent, and connected to others.

- The good life can be taught.

And more beautiful still is that joy and stress cannot coexist. That's right—when you are happy and joyful, the stress response turns off, decreasing the production of all those harmful stress hormones. Just smiling has been shown to speed the body's recovery after a stressful event. This gives even more power to having a good sense of humor!

So, positivity brings a focus to those things that make you happy. Happiness leads to good things, which lead to more good things, decreasing your stress levels. It's time to take your positive feelings more seriously!

Today, while you're at work, see how long you can maintain your happy-go-lucky attitude. If something gets you down, do something to pick yourself up. Take a short break away from your work and get outside. Skip down the sidewalk for a few steps—I bet you can't help but smile.

When you hit the break room and the topic of discussion is the same old depressing stuff, take your food somewhere else and listen to some good tunes instead. If you focus on the negative, the negative will expand into your life. If you focus on happy music or do a little happy dance, happiness will expand into your life. Isn't that a better way to spend your break?

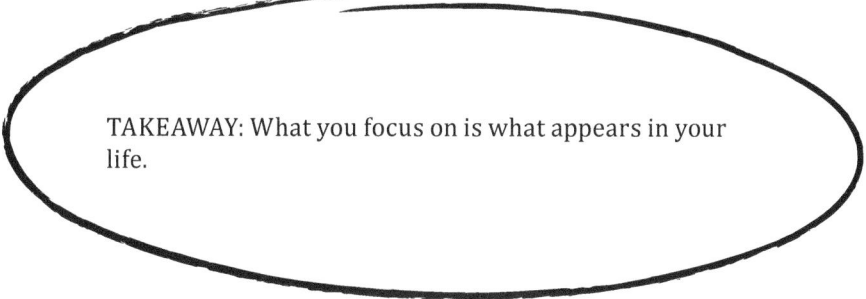

TAKEAWAY: What you focus on is what appears in your life.

Lesson 28
Change the Changeable

I have noticed even people who claim everything is predestined, and that we can do nothing to change it, look before they cross the road.
~ Stephen Hawking

God grant me the serenity to accept the things I cannot change, the courage to change the things I can, and the wisdom to know the difference.
~ Reinhold Neibuhr

Nothing is permanent. In a few billion years, even the Sun and Earth and our whole solar system will be gone! Change is the one thing you can always count on. The trouble is, when you're feeling trapped in difficult circumstances, it can seem like nothing ever changes.

Rather than nothing ever changing, it's more likely that things feel like they're not changing fast enough. This happens when you're waiting for changes to happen to you. You're waiting to react, instead of taking control and deciding how you'd like your life to look.

This is the difference between reactive and proactive living.

One of my mentors says, "Pain pushes until vision pulls," speaking to the fact that when things suck, you don't feel like you have any control in the matter; it feels like you're getting shoved here and there, relentlessly.

If you have a vision for what you want and are making daily steps in that direction, even when there are challenges, they don't drag you down.

I used to be a hardcore road-rager. Anyone who got in my way was a target. The L.A. roadways were my battleground and stupid drivers were the enemy. Going too slow? I'd tailgate them. Not taking the left turn fast enough? HONK!! Cut me off? Don't even think about it.

After years of this bad habit, I had to do some introspection to understand how to change things. Within a few weeks of making the shift toward more happiness, I stumbled on a clue.

I noticed that I always left my house for work at the very last minute. Most days, the only way I could make it on time was to aggressively speed, tailgate, and rush my way to work. This left me in a tense and angry state *before I even started my shift!*

Recognizing this madness—doing the same thing every day, hoping for a different result—I started leaving 15 minutes earlier. I took the long way. I relaxed into the drive.

My desire for a life with more happiness helped me see this little choice I could make. I shifted from knee-jerk habitual reactions (getting pushed around by pain) to proactively choosing a response that would help me get where I wanted to be (getting pulled by the vision).

You've already jotted down some ideas for where you want to be when it comes to feeling less stressed and more energized. Reflect on what you want to have in your life and decide what small choice you can make today to make it happen.

The key is to start small. Change the changeable. Get up just 10 minutes earlier and start your day with a walk outside. Read a book for 30 minutes today. Take the long way home.

Making space for more joy to flow is just a small step away.

TAKEAWAY: Changing what you *can* change shifts you toward opportunity and away from limitation.

Lesson 29
Do One Thing at a Time

The one thing that can solve most of our problems is dancing.
~ James Brown

Give whatever you are doing and whoever you are with the gift of your attention.
~ Jim Rohn

"Just take one call at a time," my supervisors would say before I was about to start another shift on the 911 lines, offering a way to (hopefully) prevent mistakes and complaints on the phones. It's actually great advice.

Taking one call at a time means that you meet the current call as if it were the first, without the years of conditioning that happens from taking thousands of calls in a career.

Great advice, but much easier said than done.

I was always amazed by a friend of mine who would meet every call to the non-emergency line with a cheery, "What are you reporting?" Smiles in her voice and all. This after nearly 30 years on the job, too!

I asked her what her secret was. I had been on the job less than three years and my annoyance with callers was already palpable.

She said that she was happy to be where she was. She enjoyed the company of her coworkers, and she took pleasure in providing whatever form of assistance she could to the person at the other end of her line.

Because she wasn't hoping for things to be different or wishing to be somewhere else, she was free to treat each caller with attention and care.

My cynical and skeptical mind thought, *Must be nice*, as I contemplated a life where I didn't have to struggle to be happy over being discontent—I could always be happy and friendly because it was my only setting!

This cynical thought is an oversimplification of what the perpetually sunny, like my friend, go through, however. She certainly could choose to focus on the drama and the difficulties above all else. But, after choosing happiness for so long, she's stuck in this mode. Isn't that a great mode to be stuck in?!

Here's a quick little experiment to help you move into the mode of "taking one call at a time" in your life. The next time you're feeling frazzled, notice how many things you have on your mind or in front of you. You only have so much willpower, and then you need to recharge.

A surefire method to get a break between thoughts and recharge is to use the 5-5-5 breathing method.

It goes like this: Inhale for a count of five. Hold for a count of five. Exhale for a count of five. Repeat that ten times. In fact, go ahead and recharge right now.

Whether you're at your desk or sitting at home put everything aside—your magazines, books, crocheting, playing cards—everything, including this book.

For the next 5-10 minutes, do just one thing. Sit there and tend to each thing in your life with the utmost attention. Between activities, notice your breath or your thoughts or just relax your body.

Use the 5-5-5 method any time you have a window of opportunity. Between activities or projects. When you're in your car. When you're in line at the grocery store.

Notice how you can "take one call at a time" wherever you are today.

TAKEAWAY: Do just one thing whenever you can for less distraction and less stress.

Part 4

Avoiding the Traps

Lesson 30
Stay Out of Your Thinking Traps

The world we have created is a product of our thinking; it cannot be changed without changing our thinking.
~ Albert Einstein

Begin challenging your own assumptions. Your assumptions are your windows to the world. Scrub them off every once in a while, or the light won't come in.
~ Alan Alda

Creating some space around your unconscious, and usually reflexive, thought processes is a good way to introduce more relaxation into your life. It provides openness needed for your transformation, your paradigm shift.

Once you enter that world of your thought processes, you will probably find that you have less control than you think. So many of your thoughts are just habitual. You've reached the point where you're on autopilot just making the same decisions over and over.

You may have irrational thinking patterns or have a tendency to think in stressful ways all of the time. Certain patterns of thinking are so entrenched that you don't even realize you have them.

Thankfully, the process of bringing them to the surface is relatively painless. Once you realize you have them, it becomes easier to deal with them.

There are ten primary patterns of irrational thinking we fall into. Which one(s) do you see in yourself?

1. **Black and white thinking:** "It's all or nothing. I have to do things perfectly, because anything less is a failure."

2. **Disqualifying the positives:** "Life feels like one disappointment after another."

3. **Negative self-labeling:** "I feel like a failure. I'm flawed. If people knew the real me, they wouldn't like me."

4. **Catastrophizing:** "If something is going to happen, it'll probably be the worst case scenario."

5. **Mind reading:** "I can tell people don't like me because of the way they behave."

6. **Should statements:** "I should've done better." "People should act differently."

7. **Excessive need for approval:** "I can only be happy if people like me. If someone is upset, it's probably my fault."

8. **Disqualifying the present:** "I'll relax later. First I have to rush to finish this."

9. **Dwelling on pain:** "If I dwell on why I'm unhappy and think about what went wrong, I'll figure things out and feel better."

10. **Pessimism:** "Life is a struggle." "The chips are stacked against me." "Those people have it better."

These thinking traps block the opportunity for change. Negativity brings on more negative thoughts, and then you feel stuck.

Breaking out of the trap and into a space of possibility takes a bit of practice, and the next lesson offers a specific exercise for doing it.

> TAKEAWAY: Identifying your habitual thinking helps to change your thoughts and decrease your stress.

Lesson 31
The Daily Thought Record

Thoughts are shadows of our feelings—
always darker, emptier, simpler.
~ Friedrich Nietzsche

Such as are your habitual thoughts,
such also will be the character of your mind;
for the soul is dyed by the thoughts.
~ Marcus Aurelius

When an event happens in your life that causes an automatic cascade of negative thinking, which then causes a negative response, there's no space between the event and response. The event and response happen together, causing a negative outcome.

Remember, E + R = O? Between the Event and your Response to the Event there is an opportunity to create space. With space, you can choose a new Response.

When stressed or anxious, thoughts and feelings can swirl in your mind and seem overwhelming. Putting them down on paper helps you sort it all out and see things more clearly. The daily thought record takes about 15 minutes each day.

Daily Thought Record Exercise

1. Start by identifying a situation you wish you handled better. Write the details of this situation down on a sheet of paper.

2. Looking at the situation, what thought first popped into your mind? This is probably an automatic thought you've had before. Now check the list in the previous lesson for the irrational pattern behind the thought.

3. Now, see if you can source the negative belief. Did this thinking come from a particular situation or person? Is there a deep belief or fear driving your thinking? Write this down.

4. The next step is to challenge your thinking. Look for evidence both for and against the thought pattern. Be sure to see the whole picture. If your thinking trap is "disqualifying the positives," and you feel like things never go your way, take a step back even further to identify a moment where things actually did go your way.

5. Consider the consequences. What are the short-term and long-term consequences if you continue to think like this? Always thinking badly about yourself or your situation takes a gradual toll. What is the impact? Once you understand your negative thought pattern, you can shift into a healthier way of thinking.

6. What's an alternative way to think about this situation? Now, write down a positive belief and an affirmation that reflects these healthier thoughts.

7. What action can you take in the future to support your new thinking?

8. Now notice if you feel slightly better or optimistic. This step reaffirms that by changing your thinking you can change your mood. Awesome!

Using this method as a daily practice for 30 days has been shown to make healthier thought patterns a more regular part of your day.

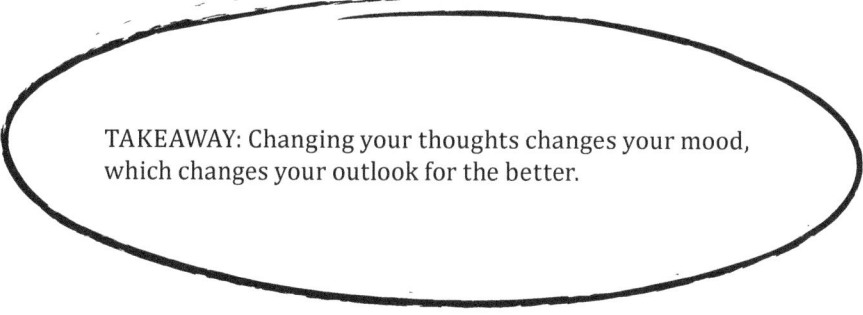

TAKEAWAY: Changing your thoughts changes your mood, which changes your outlook for the better.

Lesson 32
Silence Your Inner Critic

Talk to yourself like you would to someone you love.
~ Brene Brown

Be careful how you are talking to yourself because you are listening.
~ Lisa M. Hayes

You feel the way you think. Don't think so? Have you ever gotten into a heated argument with someone and woken up the next morning with the exchange still lingering in your head? Like a dark cloud blocking out the sun, these thoughts can take you away from the brightness of the moment as you brood over what was said.

The best way to feel good, then, is to mind your thoughts.

A little self-criticism is a good thing. It can provide the motivation to improve some area of life, but excessive self-criticism can backfire. "I need to work out more" is much different than "I'm fat and ugly." When the criticism is particularly harsh, you get stuck. It's hard to see what actions to take when any action seems like it will only bring you more of the same.

What is the inner critic? It's that voice inside your head that wants you to be better, the part of you that is continually seeking to improve. Your inner critic started out with good intentions.

On another level, your inner critic can erode confidence, prevent you from doing the things you want to do, and help push you to burnout.

Other popular negative thoughts offered by the inner critic include:

- "There's something wrong with you."
- "You're not good enough."
- "You're different from other people."
- "No one ever notices you."

How can you tell the difference between your inner critic and your true self? Notice how you feel when your inner critic kicks in. Do you feel a slight drop in energy or a tightness in your stomach or chest? It could mean that your inner critic is preventing you from seeing a better way of doing things.

Use this 4-step process to overcome your inner critic and start feeling good today:

Step 1. Identify what your inner critic is telling you. Acknowledge that this thought process is separate from your real point of view and that this thought loop is not a reflection of reality.

Step 2. To further differentiate yourself from the inner critic, write down these thoughts in the second person (as "you" statements). For example, a thought like "I can't get anything right. I'll never be successful," should be written as "You can't get anything right. You'll never be successful." Notice how hostile and untrue these "You" statements are.

Step 3. Respond to your inner critic by writing down a more realistic and compassionate viewpoint of yourself. "You always mess up," could be written as, "I may make mistakes, but I'm always improving." This isn't to build up your ego but to show yourself a kinder, more honest attitude.

Step 4. Don't act on the directives of your inner critic. Focus on who you are and what you aim to achieve. If your inner critic gets louder, telling you to play small or not take chances, then play big and take chances.

As you get into the practice of refuting the untrue words of the inner critic and ignoring what this voice says, the voice gets smaller and smaller, affecting you less and less, paving the way to unconditional happiness.

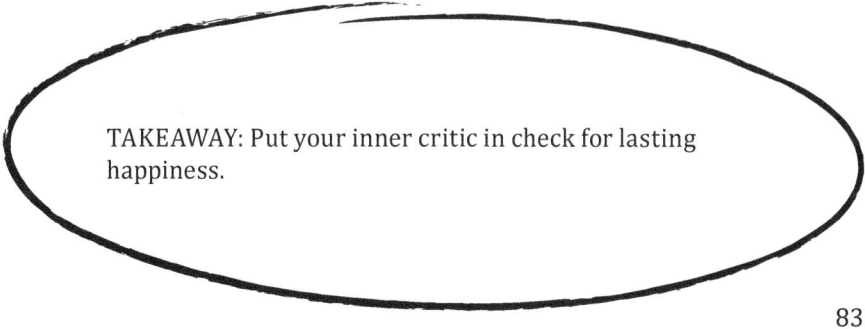

TAKEAWAY: Put your inner critic in check for lasting happiness.

Lesson 33
You Can If You Think You Can

*What lies behind us and what lies before us
are tiny matters compared to what lies within us.*
~ Ralph Waldo Emerson

*Self-esteem is as important to our well-being as legs
are to a table. It is essential for physical and
mental health and for happiness.*
~ Louise Hart

Do you remember the excitement and nervousness that accompanied going into the next grade in school, especially the first day of high school? High school! Would you cut the mustard? Would your old group of friends still be together? What would the teachers be like? So many questions...so many unknowns.

And yet, as the first few days of classes got underway, you realized the same thing as every other year: You already had all the basic tools necessary for success; the next grade was the next step in your learning journey.

Outside of school, the steps of achievement are a bit less clear—you don't have grade levels to measure your progress—but one thing remains the same: Life only presents you with what you can handle. The path before you offers the very next step in the journey.

There are times, however, when you feel like you can't handle it. You can't deal with the stress. The feelings of burnout are just too much. You don't want to get out of bed. You can't seem to get anything right.

Of course you have bad days, but you can bounce back from them more quickly, and increase your chances of having more and more good days by enhancing your level of self-esteem. Those with high self-esteem are more likely to feel that they have control over their happiness and that they can succeed.

Self-esteem and anxiety are closely related. If you have low self-esteem, you will perceive a greater number of situations as threatening, and respond accordingly (fight or flight). If you have high self-esteem, you will rarely feel threatened by your circumstances and get involved in a larger range of activities.

One of the keys to reducing your stress levels is to raise your level of self-esteem. With greater self-esteem you can also count on feeling less anxious. A powerful way to boost self-esteem is to get into the practice of reflecting on the things you've accomplished in life. Even if you're someone who likes to say, "I haven't accomplished anything worth mentioning," there are notable experiences that you've overlooked. I guarantee it.

A friend of mine said that very thing to me. "I've lived such a boring life, I haven't done anything!" she lamented. Yet she's raised two of the kindest, gentlest, most attentive, and caring kids I know.

While it may seem to some like a stretch for her to tout raising wonderful children as a major accomplishment, this road was dotted with specific moments where she chose to honor her high value for parenthood. Being available every day after school is a huge accomplishment!

Looking back at your life, what experiences of perseverance, determination, love, or generosity are you proud of? Write down these accomplishments on a blank sheet of paper. Make the list long enough that you feel the warm fuzzies of achievement in your chest, stomach, or wherever they swell up for you.

This is the feeling of confidence, of high self-esteem. Return to it often. Make a practice of drawing strength from your past accomplishments, and more confidence will come of it.

If you were to dwell in this state of confidence each day, how would your life be different?

TAKEAWAY: Confidence is always accessible when you see how far you've come.

Lesson 34
Know the Power of Your Will

People do not lack strength, they lack will.
~ Victor Hugo

*The best day of your life is the one on which you decide your life is your own.
No apologies or excuses. No one to lean on, rely on, or blame. The gift is yours—
it is an amazing journey—and you alone are responsible for the quality of it.
This is the day your life really begins.*
~ Bob Moawad

Did you know that you have a limited supply of willpower available to you each day? That's right. Willpower is an exhaustible resource.

As Gary Keller put it in his book, *The One Thing: The Surprisingly Simple Truth Behind Extraordinary Results*, "The more we use our mind, the less minding power we have. Willpower is like a fast-twitch muscle that gets tired and needs a rest." If you get a good night's sleep, you wake up in the morning with a full charge. As the day wears on, you become less able to summon the will to act outside of your default actions.

Looking at the moments in your day that deplete willpower illustrates why it's so hard for you to make changes, even though such changes would be good for your health.

Things that use up your willpower include:
- Filtering distractions
- Resisting temptation

- Suppressing emotion
- Restraining aggression
- Suppressing impulses
- Doing something you don't enjoy
- Coping with fear
- Multitasking

Any time you encounter a situation at work that causes you to take one of the above actions, it saps a bit of your willpower, making it unavailable later in the day.

This is why you get home and find it nearly impossible to muster up the strength to exercise, even though you might like to; why it's so hard to stop eating junk food, even though you don't want to do it anymore; why you keep saying "Yes" to the people and things you'd rather say "No" to.

You're forced to settle for your old default settings because you don't have the willpower to do otherwise.

Knowing this, you have to time your actions accordingly. To get the results you want and to make the changes necessary for more happiness and less burnout, you need to act when you have the available willpower, when you're fresh. What time of day is that for you?

Schedule challenging tasks during your peak time. Get up a little earlier and go for a 10-minute walk. Make a conscious effort to take your break away from your desk or outside your office.

You need to intentionally take downtime to replenish your stores of energy and willpower. If you have to jump right into your housework after a 12-hour shift, take 10 minutes to lie down or sit quietly beforehand to regroup. Ask the family for help. Be gentle and kind with yourself in any way you can.

If you don't, chances are good that you'll break down...which will bring you downtime that you can't really enjoy.

TAKEAWAY: Use your willpower, when you have it, to make the changes you'd most like to see.

Lesson 35
Letting Go of the Hassles

If you break your neck, if you have nothing to eat, if your house is on fire, then you've got a problem. Everything else is inconvenience.
~ Robert Fulghum

In this life we will encounter hurts and trials that we will not be able to change; we are just going to have to allow them to change us.
~ Ron Lee Davis

The truth is, most of what you deal with each day is small stuff.

Even when you bring your home life into the mix, things are pretty much on an even keel. But you don't always act calmly. Like when you have a disagreement or a challenging exchange with a coworker, you have a tendency to flip out when the little things get to you.

Like the saying goes, "Don't sweat the small stuff, and it's all small stuff."

The stressful aspects of your day can be summed up as *daily hassles* or *major life events*.

Daily hassles include traffic, chores, coworkers, clients, and the like.

Major life events include the death of a loved one, a divorce or marriage, a family illness.

Noting the difference between these types of stressors, it's interesting to see which of these causes more stress. You tend to experience less stress as a result of major life events, while daily hassles tend to get under your skin. Why is this?

When you encounter a major life event, such as the death of a family member, you may grieve for a time, but you don't get worked up over it. There is an element of surrender and acceptance built in to these occurrences. You aren't feeling threatened. You generally don't go into fight or flight mode.

With daily hassles, on the other hand, you wish things were different, but have a hard time accepting that they aren't different. There's traffic—again!—and you sit there, red-faced, cursing the cars in front of you. Another demanding friend, relative, or customer takes you to that place, and it's hard to let it go.

Observing your own tendency to get riled at the small stuff, you can catch yourself focusing on the small stuff. Right then. In that moment. Instead of launching into a litany of "Why me?" pity-party thoughts, you can stop.

Begin to see how much power the hassles have over you.

If you can't change it, just let the thoughts go. This idea of surrender and acceptance isn't about being passive or weak.

On the contrary, imagine if you were able to meet the challenges of your day with an unshakeable steadiness and calm.

Instead of riding a roller coaster each day, you can choose to walk the middle path, unswayed by the small stuff that arises, staying away from the extremes of reaction and resignation.

Hassles may still arise, but instead of seeing them as hassles, they're simply things that come up, you take notice, and then they go away. No problem.

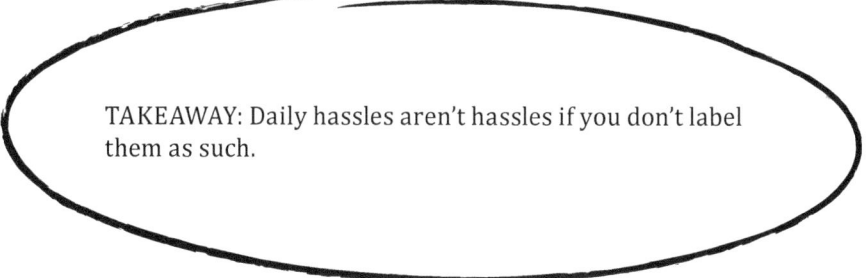

TAKEAWAY: Daily hassles aren't hassles if you don't label them as such.

Part 5

Making the Physical Shift

Lesson 36
Eliminate the Stress-Promoting Diet

*The more you eat, the less flavor;
the less you eat, the more flavor.*
~ Chinese proverb

*Life expectancy would grow by leaps and bounds
if green vegetables smelled as good as bacon.*
~ Doug Larsen

Most of what we've spoken about has been centered on the inner game of less stress. Positivity, happiness, the ability to relax, and healthy relationships all make a huge difference, and, when combined with a body that is nourished, you become automatically more resilient and joyful.

Burnout seems to be primarily a mental phenomenon, but as you've seen, you feel how you think. This also works the other way around. You think how you feel. If you feel lousy every day because you have eaten nothing but junk food and empty calories for weeks, this affects your outlook. The mind-body connection is either working for you or against you.

The following three strategies can help fortify your body's defenses against the wear and tear of chronic stress:

Strategy 1. Adjust your diet during stressful times. Go fresh for less stress.

When your stress levels are high, eating complex carbohydrates, such as fruits, vegetables, whole grains, and beans helps stimulate serotonin production in the brain. Serotonin enhances feelings of well-being and calm. Avoid carbohydrates with fats and sugar as they prevent the production of this "feel-good" hormone.

Strategy 2. Reduce the consumption of stress-promoting foods. Give yourself the gift of nourishment.

Caffeine, sugar, and salt are examples of foods that can turn on the stress response or hinder the body's systems. Did you know that the amount of caffeine in one Starbucks coffee is enough to increase blood pressure, cause an uptick in heart rate, and put you on edge?

In measured doses, this can be OK. However, when you're wired on caffeine (also found in tea and soda) for too long, anxiety, irritability, irregular heartbeat, and an inability to concentrate can result. Caffeine has a half-life of 8 hours, so even within 8 hours after your last cup of coffee your sleep quality can be affected. Try decreasing your caffeine intake by drinking green tea instead.

Processed flours and refined white sugars, while making tasty treats, are completely devoid of the vitamins and nutrients you need to be your best in stressful times. When you're stressed, the body uses up B-vitamins and, when they're not available, you feel run down.

Strategy 3. Reduce fat consumption. Eat light to feel and think lighter.

The typical Western diet is made up of 40-50% fat, without much in the way of fruits and vegetables. A better diet mix includes 10-15% fat, 70-75% carbohydrate, and 10-15% protein. Fat substitute products, like low-fat ice cream, cheese, milk and other low-fat options don't change eating habits. To decrease fat intake, you have to make a concerted effort to do so.

Aside from giving the body what it needs to thrive, eating a stress-reducing diet helps you feel better in your skin overall. Feeling better in your body enhances well-being, giving you an extra boost.

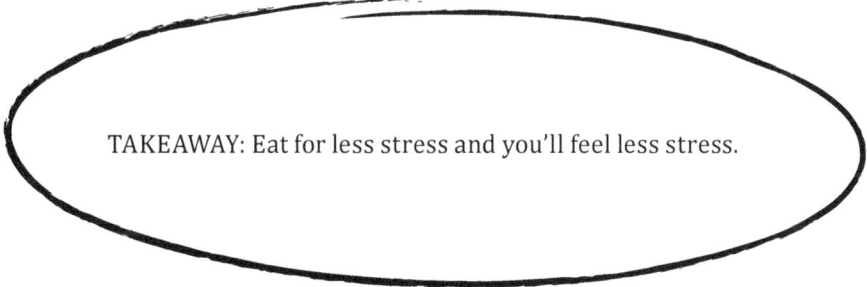

TAKEAWAY: Eat for less stress and you'll feel less stress.

Lesson 37
Reduce Your Stress with Exercise

*Those who think they have no time for exercise
will sooner or later have to find time for illness.*
~ Edward Stanley

*Physical fitness is not only one of the most important
keys to a healthy body, it is the basis of
dynamic and creative intellectual activity.*
~ John F. Kennedy

When our ancient ancestors roamed the plains searching for food, and they met a wolf or some other threat, physical activity was the natural response to this stress—fight or flight.

Now, when you get stressed, you continue to sit where you are, raised blood pressure and all, stewing in the pressure.

The body is designed to take action when stressed, and when you exercise, you receive the many benefits of this activity. Exercise is one of the simplest and most effective means of stress reduction and it is the natural outlet for the body during its fight or flight state of arousal. After exercise, the body returns to its normal equilibrium, and you feel relaxed and refreshed.

It's not surprising that an unfit person might not handle stress as well as one who is fit and in good condition. When confronted with stress, the body undergoes a number of changes. More oxygen is required, the heart rate increases, muscles tense, and blood pressure increases.

Exercise improves and develops your capacity to handle stressful events. It increases production of endorphins, the body's feel-good drugs. It provides a safety valve for stress, helps shed unwanted pounds, and improves cardiovascular efficiency and metabolism. It also fights chronic fatigue and insomnia.

I know what you're thinking: *On top of all this, now I have to turn into a fitness freak, too?!*

No, you don't. I see so many people adopt an all-or-nothing mentality around exercise and fitness that prevents them from doing anything at all.

You don't have to start training for a marathon. You don't have to run. You don't have to compare yourself to others or to your old high-school self.

Research has shown that just 10 minutes of walking each day is enough to stimulate blood flow and allow you to begin enjoying all of the positive benefits of exercise that you've heard about. Commit to taking 10 minutes to walk each day for the next 2 weeks and see how you feel. You can always go back to the way things were.

When exercising, it's important to focus on the rewards.

You'll feel more relaxed, energized, and refreshed; you'll be better able to concentrate; and your sleep will improve. Try tracking your exercise activity. That which gets tracked can be managed.

With just a moderate amount of exercise, you can stave off the effects of stress and cure yourself of the dreaded "sitting disease." Yes, sitting disease. The American Cancer Society published a study in 2010 that followed over 123,000 people from 1993 to 2006. The study found that women who were inactive and sat for over six hours a day were 94% more likely to die younger than those who were physically active and sat less than three hours a day. Crazy! Men who were inactive were 48% more likely to die younger.

TAKEAWAY: Get up and get active. You'll prevent stress, stop the sitting disease, and be happier.

Lesson 38
Be a Sleeping Beauty

*Without enough sleep,
we all become tall two-year-olds.*
~ JoJo Jensen

*The amount of sleep required by the average person
is five minutes more.*
~ Wilson Mizner

Sleep is one of the most undervalued aspects of life. You drink coffee to compensate for not getting enough sleep, and then you take sleeping pills because you're so stressed that you can't get to sleep when your head hits the pillow. Lack of sleep has been shown to result in fatigue, sugar cravings, energy crashes in the afternoon, and overeating.

Long hours and demands outside of work put more pressure on your sleep-deprived body and mind; you become prone to mistakes and grumpiness. This leads to more stress.

Research shows that getting less than 8 hours of sleep each night can lead to a decline in cognitive functioning later in life, and those suffering from insomnia are at 3 times the risk for all diseases.

So, if stress increases the risk of disease, and lack of sleep triples the risk of disease, where does that leave us? With a great reason to get more sleep!

But how? There are only 24 hours in a day!

Here are a few tips for getting the sleep you need:

1. **Make it a commitment.** Since you have coffee and other ways to help you burn the candle at both ends, sleep can seem like the easiest thing to sacrifice when you need extra hours. Unfortunately, the days add up, and you push yourself deep into the red zone. Prioritizing sleep is the first big step in reclaiming your health and vivacity.

2. **Get into a rhythm.** Establish a regular sleep schedule. Because your body prefers routine, you have to stick to a regular hour of going to bed and rising. This helps regulate your melatonin and cortisol levels for the best rest.

3. **Develop a bedtime routine.** To wind down for good quality sleep, try the following activities:

    - Five minutes of writing in a notebook (or journal), answering the questions, "What 3 things went well today? What is 1 thing I can grow from?"
    - Thirty minutes of reading
    - Fifteen minutes of mindfulness meditation practice or focused breathing

4. **Reduce caffeine intake in the afternoon.** Caffeine activates the stress response and can take more than 8 hours to leave the system. You may feel sleepy in the afternoon, but once you get off work, you'll get that boost that will take you the next few hours until bedtime.

5. **Track your sleep.** When you have a goal of getting more and better sleep, it helps to keep a sleep journal to track the length, quality, and other factors that may be contributing to your sleep cycle. Especially when you're tired, the days just blur together, and you may not be aware of how poorly you've been sleeping the past few nights. Writing it down allows you to see it right there in front of you. Many fitness trackers also track your sleep, which can help you understand your sleep patterns very clearly.

6. **Designate a "sleep-in day"!** Take one day each week where you get to linger between the sheets.

TAKEAWAY: Getting enough sleep is one of the most powerful ways to reduce stress levels.

Lesson 39
Laugh Whenever You Can

With the fearful strain that is on me night and day, if I did not laugh I should die.
~ Abraham Lincoln

And keep a sense of humor. It doesn't mean you have to tell jokes. If you can't think of anything else, when you're my age, take your clothes off and walk in front of a mirror. I guarantee you'll get a laugh.
~ Art Linkletter

Stress and joy cannot coexist. It's impossible. When you're engaged in belly laughter, having a good time, the stress response is shut down. Because it reduces stress, laughter positively affects all aspects of being. Just smiling has been shown to lower stress levels.

Physiologically, laughter enhances your natural defenses against illness.

Mentally, it enhances problem-solving skills and offers new perspectives.

Emotionally, it elevates mood and counteracts depression symptoms.

Socially, laughter fosters better communication and improves cooperation and empathy between people.

Spiritually, it helps you build resilience to stress and teaches you to live and be at peace with others.

Laughter truly is the best medicine, as the old column in *Reader's Digest* always told us. The problem is, while we do laugh on the job, it's not nearly enough. We're so serious! And if you've ever been the butt of a joke, the target of bullies, or on the receiving end of ill-willed sarcasm, you know that there's a difference between being laughed at and laughed with. So the type of humor counts, too.

How can you invite more positive humor into your life? Here are a few things that will help you bust a gut and reap the rewards of lightening up a bit.

- Love your smile and love your laugh. Don't be afraid to show the world your smiling face and laugh out loud. I had one friend who would cover her mouth or keep her smile small because she didn't like her teeth. Another would hold back his laugh because he thought it sounded dorky.

- Seek out the funny. Spend time with funny people. Make it a daily task to laugh. YouTube, your pet, your funny friend, a comedy night—whatever! Pleasure-seeking is not a sometimes thing. Balance the seriousness of your work with the lightness of laughter.

- Play pretend. Do you remember building forts, going on expeditions in the back woods, or exploring with friends when you were a kid? Time disappeared, fun was the currency, and we had no choice but to be right where we were. Give yourself permission to play this week and tap into that childlike wonder again.

Laughter and good humor are infectious, just like negativity. Which would you like more of? Making it a point to counteract challenging moments in your day with a little levity is a practice that can change the overall tone of your entire day, week, or month.

TAKEAWAY: Laughter is a gateway to greater relaxation, better communication, and fun times with good people.

Part 6

Living Your New Reality

Lesson 40
With a Little Help from My Friends

*The strong individual is the one who
asks for help when he needs it.*
~ Rona Barrett

*Asking for help does not mean that we are weak
or incompetent. It usually indicates an
advanced level of honesty and intelligence.*
~ Anne Wilson Schaef

If you're a nurturing caregiver to the world, you rarely ask for help. You don't want to burden family or friends with things, and you think that they wouldn't really understand the work you do anyway. So you tend to keep things close.

When it comes to help with decreasing your stress levels, asking for assistance can be even more difficult. You're supposed to be able to handle the pressure—you're a professional, after all.

The beautiful thing is, the journey away from chronic stress and burnout happens more quickly when you enroll your family and friends in the effort.

In Lesson 21, I talked about Laura, the dispatcher of 12 years who finally asked her family for help around the house, but only after being taken out by an illness. Laura's breakthrough was that she didn't have to do it all alone.

This realization made a huge impact on her overall level of happiness. She looked more relaxed and she smiled more. How cool!

Here's a quick way to enroll your family in your effort:

Take out a blank sheet of paper and brainstorm ten ways your family (spouse, kids, brothers, sisters, mom, dad) can help you achieve your vision of less stress. This could include delegation of duties around the house, having someone check in with you occasionally, or meeting weekly to share your progress.

I meet weekly with my brother via Skype (he lives in Singapore). We hold each other accountable to goals in the areas of fitness and business success.

The people you spend the most time with have a huge impact on how you act and live. Highlighting this fact, legendary motivational speaker Jim Rohn said, "You are the average of the five people you spend the most time with."

If all your friends are stressed and angry, chances are good that you feel similarly. Does your break time at work ever turn into one big gripe session? Like one that you need to get away from before it infects you, too? Been there.

Here's a quick way to see how your circle of friends affects you:

Write down the five friends that you spend the most time with. Ask yourself a few questions about them. Who are they? What do they do with their time? Do they add to your stress level, or do they help with it?

Be honest with yourself as you look at this. Your tendency may be to cut people some slack—especially old friends—because they've been in your life for so long.

Just like any toxic relationship, toxic friendships can also prevent you from getting where you want to be.

Once you see who in your life is on the same wavelength with your new vision, set the intention to spend more time with them, or at least be more conscious of how much time you spend with these people versus those who aren't helping.

TAKEAWAY: When the people in your life support your efforts, you'll improve your life much more quickly.

Lesson 41
To Forgive is to Get Something Back

*Forgiveness does not change the past,
but it does enlarge the future.*
~ Paul Boese

When you hold resentment toward another, you are bound to that person or conditioned by an emotional link that is stronger than steel. Forgiveness is the only way to dissolve that link and get free.
~ Art Linkletter

Sometimes it can be hard to forgive what happens at work. Gossip, lies, unfair treatment, and insensitive communication can become magnified and trigger old stuff. Often to just get along, we must overlook pettiness, and management and organizational practices that offend, hurt, and challenge our sensibilities.

It's important to remember that often these actions, while insensitive, can be unconscious and not designed to hurt, but it's also important that we not suppress what we feel when they happen.

Rationalization has limited impact when our values are being challenged, or violated. Too often unforgiving attitudes accumulate when we attempt to bury these feelings. This can trigger old wounds and resurface unresolved grievances.

With every incident of perceived disrespect—from bosses, coworkers, drivers on the road—you throw another log on your smoldering fire of anger and bitterness. You end up bringing all of this old hurt forward, expressing it in the moment.

Answer the following ten questions to find out if you're hanging on to any bitterness:

1. Do you ever lash out at others in anger?
2. Do you replay past hurts over and over again?
3. Do you have a sour outlook on life?
4. Do you find it difficult to say you're sorry or ask forgiveness?
5. Do you expect that others will let you down?
6. Is it difficult to smile?
7. Is it difficult to sleep well at night?
8. Do you often tell others how someone hurt you?
9. Are you critical and sarcastic?
10. Do you complain often throughout the day?

If you answered "Yes" to at least two of these questions, there is a good chance that you are angry or bitter and could invite some forgiveness into your life for less stress. Being in a state of "unforgiveness" saps your energy, monopolizes your thoughts, and keeps you stuck in the past.

Forgiveness allows a break from this past and frees up your energy to be more present here and now. And since the work you do is unforgiving at times, it would be nice to have more energy to meet these challenges, wouldn't it?

One of the most helpful perspectives to adopt when it comes to forgiveness is that most of what you endure at the hands of others isn't personal. At all. When someone chooses to lash out, their reaction is about them. When a coworker says something rude, that approach is on them.

Seeing this, you can take a step back. It's hard to step back when you're personally and emotionally involved. When it's not personal, the emotions become less intense, and you can think more clearly.

In this space, you can extend forgiveness to the person or situation that has created difficulty for you, disconnecting from the negative feelings you associate with it. Taking a deep breath, you can let go even more.

TAKEAWAY: Forgive everyone. What they do to you isn't personal, and it only harms you to hold a grudge.

Lesson 42
Don't Take Work Home

Those who play rarely become brittle in the face of stress or lose the healing capacity for humor.
~ Stuart Brown, M.D.

Work consists of whatever a body is obliged to do. Play consists of whatever a body is not obliged to do
~ Mark Twain

Being resilient, choosing happiness over discontentment, and giving from the overflow requires the act of balancing. You balance your work life against your personal life. You balance the joyful times with the stressful times. Life really is about contrast.

If you don't counterbalance the "work mode" of life with ample doses of play, you burn out. You need to recharge; downtime away from work is the key. This balancing act, if to be effective, must involve a clear separation between work time and play time.

How good are you at leaving work at work? Do you take work home with you, or are you able to leave a good day's work done? Even if you don't physically take work home with you, you may feel unable to turn off the work mindset.

If you're taking on the stress of the job in the form of tension, a bad attitude, and trauma, you're not leaving the work at work.

So, you have to make a break from this mindset to leave work at work. This takes a little practice.

When you're done with work, let it go.

Step outside of the building, take a deep breath and, as you exhale, imagine your biggest worry from the day melting away. Shake out your arms a bit and just feel the energies of the day falling off.

On your drive home, continue to allow the distance to increase. You can imagine work's challenges just fading until they're gone.

As you near your house, allow the pace of your thinking to slow down a bit. If your day consists of multitasking, fast-thinking, and moving quickly, try to do the opposite. Focus on one thing at a time and move more slowly.

Entering your home, see if you can continue to maintain this slower pace. Resist getting swept up in the stream of your responsibilities.

On your day off, don't cram your day with a to-do list that can never be completed. This demanding, fast-paced mindset is work. Schedule a block of time to do something fun. Give yourself permission to play. (For great strategies on handling your to-do list, see Dr. Joe Serio's book, *Time Management: 50 Lessons on Finding Time for What's Important*.)

Choose a play activity that calls to your childlike wonder. When was the last time you took yourself on a date? This may sound funny, but giving back to yourself is the best way to replenish what's lost in the hustle and bustle of a busy week.

When you're at work, be there. When you're playing, just play. Take a break from the mindset that causes you stress, and the stress will stop.

What will you do to play on your next day off?

TAKEAWAY: Play is the key to balancing the demands of your job.

Lesson 43
Get a Life

A hobby a day keeps the doldrums away.
~ Phyllis McGinley

You can be childlike without being childish.
A child always wants to have fun. Ask yourself,
'Am I having fun?'
~ Christopher Meloni

Inspiration's biggest enemy is boredom. You may get excited about adopting a new outlook, using new methods to reduce your stress, and having more fun, but if your current mix of activities includes the same old stuff, then you're just a few days away from falling right back into the same old rut.

To keep the inspiration flowing, you need to be excited about the life you're living.

Your job may provide this for you at times. So often, though, after doing this for years—decades—you're looking to retirement to save you.

Why does the next day off, the next vacation, or retirement sound so enticing? Because you're bored of what you're doing. The stressed mind gets dull.

The problem with looking to the next day off to cure this boredom is that it doesn't cure it. The boredom follows you wherever you go. Just because you have time off doesn't mean you'll magically come up with exciting new things to do to fill your time.

You've done the wake up—go to work—go home—go to sleep cycle so many times without any variation that you don't know what you want to do besides this. So you watch TV, drink, or smoke without considering whether this is something you actually *want* and *love* to do.

It's time to get a life outside of work. Right now. Not "when I retire." Not "someday." Now.

I'm inviting you to try something new, to stretch your comfort zone a little bit. What's something you've always wanted to do but have been waiting for the "right" time to do it?

Write it down. Now go online and find out where you can do this thing. What an amazing thing about modern life! No matter where you are, if you want something, you can just Google it and find out how to get it.

The point of this exercise is to give you something to look forward to. If you're burnt out, stressed, and miserable, the job ain't doin' it for you anymore. It's time to seek something new.

You have an almost unlimited to capacity to learn new things at any age. You simply have to take the initiative.

Can't teach an old dog new tricks? Nonsense.

The things you look forward to are the beacons that give you the spark to go to work, even when it's rough.

You work to live, not live to work, and it's your responsibility to have inspiring things to live *for.*

What are yours?

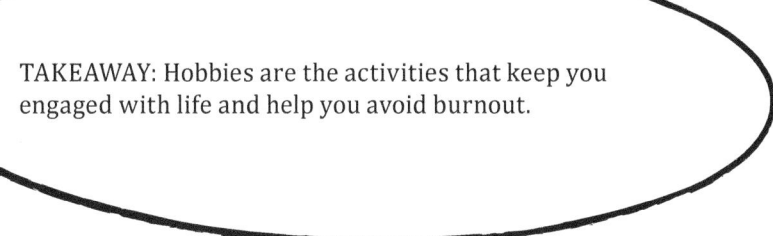

TAKEAWAY: Hobbies are the activities that keep you engaged with life and help you avoid burnout.

Lesson 44
Re-discovery

There came a time when the risk to remain right in the bud was more painful than the risk it took to blossom.
~ Anais Nin

You have to leave the city of your comfort and go into the wilderness of your intuition. What you'll discover will be wonderful. What you'll discover is yourself.
~ Alan Alda

The last two lessons asked you to have some fun. To play more. To pick up a new (or old) hobby. This might've caused some anxiety. You may have thought, *Whatever.* It's more likely that you felt regret. Regret that you've forgotten how to have fun.

In my coaching sessions, one of the first assignments I give my clients is to go out and do something fun they've forgotten about. Almost always, the first response is, "I don't know what that is. Isn't that sad? I don't know how to have fun anymore."

After some gentle coaxing, they remember. One client remembered that she always enjoyed taking her dog for a walk up to a ridge where she would watch the sunrise. Another remembered how much joy she received from having tea with an old friend.

This is simple stuff. I'm not talking about enrolling for your master's degree or jumping out of an airplane (unless that's what's really calling to you). It's about renewing your awareness of the little things that bring you joy and recommitting to doing them again.

Lost in the hustle and bustle, you put everyone else's needs before your own, not knowing that, as the years pass, you lose a bit more of yourself.

I believe this is at the core of chronic stress and burnout. You stop feeding yourself and eventually lose sight of the little pleasures. Just like it only takes five minutes of deep breathing to turn off the stress response and relax, it only takes a small bit of devotion to what you really want in order to re-awaken a zest for life.

To dust off the part of you that is looking to feel alive again, ask yourself the following four questions. It's important, however, that you don't overthink these. Go quickly, without hesitation. The first, most immediate answer is the correct one. This is your intuition speaking.

1. What does having fun look like for me?

2. How would it feel to have fun like this?

3. What's holding me back from doing this?

4. When will I take this time for myself?

Once you have the answers, it's important to honor yourself and go for it. If it involves other people, get in touch with them. Set it up. If there's something holding you back, how can you address this? Is it really an obstacle, or is it just an old thought pattern?

The stressed mind looks out into the world and sees lack and limitation. No time for play, only time to work. After years of engaging life in this way, it all feels like work. These little moments offer a break in the clouds. Like a brilliant beam of light shining through that one little opening, the light will illuminate the pathway forward.

TAKEAWAY: Letting the spontaneous and fun-loving side of you have some fun is the surest way to find relief.

Lesson 45
Seeing the Connection

*Learn how to see. Realize that
everything connects to everything else.*
~ Leonardo daVinci

*Pull a thread here and you'll find
it's attached to the rest of the world.*
~ Nadeem Aslam

Imagine that your life is a wheel. On this wheel there are five spokes, one spoke for each of the five primary areas of your life:

1. Work
2. Health
3. Relationships
4. Personal interests/hobbies
5. Spirit

Work is what you do to put bread on the table. *Health* is how you feel in your body and the actions you take to maintain good health. *Relationships* are your family and friends. *Personal interests/hobbies* are the things you do outside of work. *Spirit* is your connection to something greater than you. Religion and spiritual practice are often connected to this area, but not necessarily.

As you live your life, if you neglect one of these areas for too long, that spoke begins to weaken. But you continue to drive on the wheel. The more the spoke weakens, the bumpier the ride gets. The spoke continues to weaken, and instead of slowing down to take a look at why the ride is so bumpy, you give it more gas.

Now you're picking up speed, ignoring the pieces flying off the vehicle as the inevitable breakdown approaches.

Stress in one area causes stress in all areas. There is no separation and never was. You've just become really good at compartmentalizing things, hoping that you have it all under control.

Pain is the surest indication that something is ripe for change. Looking at the five areas of your life. Which is the most ready for adjustment?

A friend of mine was having a difficult time at work and it was affecting everything else. She had been put on disciplinary probation because her sales numbers were so low, and she had a growing fear that she might lose her job. Her level of anxiety had reached an all-time high.

In the midst of this, she began using the tools in this book. She took 15 minutes each day to sit in her garden and breathe quietly. She got back into her drawing and art.

Within six weeks, her anxiety subsided to the point where she didn't need to use the anti-anxiety meds she had been on for years. Taking time for hobbies outside of work helped her outlook on life to improve, and she began connecting more with customers at her job.

Within eight weeks, not only did she get off disciplinary probation, she was one of the top five in sales for her region. No more worries about work and more satisfaction across all areas of her life.

As you make subtle changes in your life outside of work, tending to your personal needs, enriching your life by having more fun, decreasing the effects of stress, and changing your perspective, these changes have no choice but to create changes on the job.

It only takes addressing the one most challenging area for the rest to begin to fall into place. When the space is allowed for it, you have a natural ability to spot the way forward.

TAKEAWAY: Improvement in one area of your life influences all other areas.

Lesson 46
Lisa Makes the Connection

*Life comes from physical survival;
but the good life comes from what we care about.*
~ Rollo May

*Resilience is all about being able to
overcome the unexpected.
Sustainability is about survival.
The goal of resilience is to thrive.*
~ Jamais Cascio

When Lisa was 18, she adopted a strict lifestyle of eating right and going to the gym religiously. Her efforts paid off—big time. She lost 135 pounds. She maintained this weight, and the regimen required, for 12 years. She worked out five to six times week, in the gym for at least two hours each workout.

To her, the dividends of her lifestyle were clear. The weight wasn't coming back, so that's all the evidence she needed. Until things started to go wrong.

After so many years of pushing so hard, Lisa's body began to break down. There had been signs along the way—chronic health complaints, family drama—but she kept her head down and stuck to the plan.

She never looked up long enough to evaluate whether her old way of living was right for her any longer. A health condition brought on by chronic stress caused her to take a sobering look at things. Her doctor diagnosed her with Hashimoto's disease.

Hashimoto's is a thyroid condition for which there is no cure. It is greatly affected by chronic stress. In fact, based on several years of working with clients diagnosed with Hashimoto's, it's clear to me that chronically high stress levels are the single biggest factor in the onset of Hashimoto's symptoms.

Because of her Hashimoto's, Lisa had to begin living differently. She started treating herself more gently, resting when she was tired, cutting out toxic relationships, taking time to read, meditate, and write in her journal.

Because there is no cure for the illness, a Hashimoto's diagnosis can feel like a death sentence to some. Aside from feeling sick all the time, depression can set in as the patient realizes that this state may be the new normal.

Lisa initially felt this depression. She dreaded the idea of being sick all the time. At only 32, she didn't want to miss out on the rest of her life. Instead of resigning, she took action and asked for help. She sought the support she needed to make the changes necessary to heal. She set her sights on remission.

In less than a year, Lisa made huge strides. Most notable was her mindset. Instead of seeing it as a death sentence, Lisa recently said that "Hashimoto's Disease is the best thing that happened to me. I didn't know I was on a self-destructive path, and now I have the opportunity to heal."

Symptoms are signposts, pointing in the direction of needed change. The true cost of chronic stress is realized when the symptoms are assessed and we ask, "Can I keep walking down this path? Can it be better?"

If the answer is, "Yes, I'd like it to be better," we have no choice but to do something about it. Lisa was forced to take action after enduring years of hardship. Years of hardship is not a prerequisite for positive change, but it's a fact that pain is a more significant motivator than pleasure.

If you know you're ready, start today.

Say "No" to something. Ask for help. Let go of your need to please. Dance to some loud music. Take the long way home. Go to the top of a hill and let out a mighty, "Yawp!"

TAKEAWAY: We must update our actions according to the life we want to live NOW.

Part 7

Creating Your Future

Lesson 47
The Vision for Tomorrow

You may not control all the events that happen to you, but you can decide not to be reduced by them.
~ Maya Angelou

A vision is not just a picture of what could be; it is an appeal to our better selves, a call to become something more.
~ Rosabeth Moss Kanter

In my workshops, I ask participants to describe what being stressed feels like to them. I call this the "stress metaphor" exercise.

"It feels like a heavy weight has been placed on my chest."

"It feels like a prison and there's no escape."

"It feels like I can never catch up—I'm always out of time."

Describing what it feels like to be stressed, especially in terms that create a scene or a feeling in your mind, is a powerful way to understand two things: Where you are and what that's like for you.

What is your relationship to stress? Does it tune you up, providing fuel to rise to the challenge, or does it weigh you down, causing you to feel run into the ground?

Try the stress metaphor exercise yourself, right now. How would you describe your relationship to stress, using comparisons like the ones above? Write this down in a notebook or a journal.

This is where you are right now and it's important to know that. But, here's a better question: What would you like instead?

I love this question. It has the power to lift you up from wherever you are and bring you into the space of possibility. This is the starting point for your compelling future vision.

To get where you want to be, use the power of visualization.

Boxing legend Muhammad Ali always stressed the importance of seeing himself victorious long before the actual fight.

As a struggling young actor, Jim Carrey used to picture himself being the greatest actor in the world.

Michael Jordan always took the last shot in his mind before he ever took one in real life.

Take out another blank sheet of paper, or open up to a blank page in your journal. Across the top of the page write, "My 6-Month Vision."

Imagine it's six months in the future, and you've taken the tools in this book and applied them to your life. Your feelings of burnout and daily stress have lessened considerably. You're not as rushed. You're less anxious and you're sleeping better. You're happy more often.

In as much detail as possible, write down what your life looks like from this viewpoint. What does it feel like to wake up in the morning? Are you more rested and energized? What do you do with your free time? How do you interact with your family and friends? What do you do for fun? What else is different?

Once you're done, put your six-month vision somewhere you won't lose it. Read it once a day, placing yourself in that vision, seeing what you would see, feeling what you would feel.

As you try on this vision of success, you will get used to what it feels like and see opportunities to make the future a reality now.

TAKEAWAY: Knowing where you are and where you're going helps you know when you get there.

Lesson 48
One Step at a Time

*The journey of a thousand miles
begins with a single step.*
~ Lao Tzu

*Do you want to know who you are? Don't ask. Act!
Action will delineate and define you.*
~ Thomas Jefferson

With an eye on what's possible, it's easier to see which steps will lead you there.

What is it about your vision that got you excited? Being able to sleep through the night? Less or no more chronic pain? The ability to slow down and be more available for your spouse and children? Having the headspace to get back to the hobbies you used to enjoy?

All of these things are not only possible, they happen quite naturally when you begin taking the steps outlined in these lessons. And it doesn't take heroic effort, either.

Small steps, taken regularly over the course of the coming days and weeks, have the ability to produce huge results.

Subtle shifts in behavior, applied consistently over time, lead to transformation.

When I started to make a change several years ago, my days were filled with tension headaches, stomach pain from ulcers, anger, and frustration that I spewed on everyone. These led to impatience, road rage, and conflict with coworkers and supervisors—things were bad!

Using the few simple techniques contained in this book in less than 20 minutes each day, these symptoms of stress lightened or disappeared within six weeks. **It took only six weeks to find relief from symptoms that took years to develop!** And I didn't take any drugs, go on work-related injury, or run away to a tropical island.

I continued to work at my job, just like I always had, but something inside of me shifted. My relationship with everything became easier.

Your entire life is a web of relationships. You have a relationship with your job, you have a relationship with your significant other and you have a relationship with your material possessions. What feeling pops up when you think of going into work tomorrow? This feeling speaks to whether the thoughts and perceptions around these relationships are positive or not.

The nature of your relationships, whether they are enjoyable, strained, or colored by some other thought, largely define your level of daily happiness. If you're unhappy in a relationship, what usually happens? Stress from just thinking about it.

You can change these relationships. One step at a time.

I know what you're thinking: *Easier said than done.*

Maybe, but it's worth a try. You can always go back to your old stressed-out ways of yesterday.

Instead, though, return to your vision of possibility. Any time the going gets tough, remind yourself why you're doing this. Take the time to picture your vision again. And then double down. Get back in the game.

Changing your relationship to the stressful things in life can seem like a daunting task, especially when it's all stressful. Years—decades—of conditioning have led you to relate to aspects of your life in a stressful way.

Luckily, it doesn't take decades, or even years, for radical transformation to happen.

TAKEAWAY: Taking consistent action one step at a time is the key to quick, profound transformation.

Lesson 49
You Know the Way

*A hero is someone who, in spite of weakness, doubt,
or not always knowing the answers,
goes ahead and overcomes anyway.*
~ Christopher Reeve

*Every day is a chance to start over. Any day
can be bad, surely, but any day can be good,
can be great, and that promise, that potential,
is a beautiful thing indeed.*
~ R.A. Salvatore

When I took a meditation class in 2010, I had no idea what would happen. I was just looking for relief from the pain I felt. I didn't have a vision for the life that was about to emerge. As I made the time to sit still, the answers came by themselves.

And I still had a choice. I could choose to continue to live like I had for years, or I could move along the new path that was appearing. I only needed to take the very next step.

This is the path of possibility, where even the challenging days are steps forward. In fact, challenges offer the best opportunity to practice.

The next time you're knee-deep in a difficult work situation, just notice how the exchange is affecting you. What feelings are you experiencing? What thoughts are surfacing? This dimension of awareness—the part of you that is observing your thoughts and feelings and the exchange all at once—is the part of you that knows the answers and the way forward.

The more you tune into this knowing, the easier it becomes to hear.

A friend of mine was one of those always-angry types on the job. Complaining about everything was her normal mode—you couldn't escape hearing her voice if she was working. She'd get all up-in-arms about something and then take a smoke break to cool off.

In mid-2011, she participated in my meditation program at the 911 dispatch center. The sessions had a profound effect on her. She started to lighten up and take responsibility for her attitude. She took more time for herself outside of work to go on little trips with her spouse and started losing weight. Sixty-five pounds later, she was like a new woman!

The first step was her saying "Yes" to the invitation to sit still. The rest was the natural unfolding of that first step.

An amazing thing happens when you give yourself permission to be who you really want to be. The answers arrive without provocation; the support you're looking for shows up in the most unexpected guise. You open yourself to possibility, and possibilities abound.

All it takes is a willingness to take the next step. No matter where you are today, you are on your path.

One of my mentors speaks of uncovering the liberating fires of wisdom in everyday experience. This is a powerful realization. Whatever you are going through is an opportunity to learn and become more of who you are.

You don't have to go on a vision quest through the desert or a spiritual journey to India to be who you've been waiting for. You have all the tools and all the answers with you now.

> TAKEAWAY: You've always known the way forward. The answers will appear if you just give them the space to. Then, take the next bold step and BE who you really are.

Lesson 50
Celebrate the Journey

*Let your joy be in your journey
—not in some distant goal.*
~ Tim Cook

*I have found that if you love life,
life will love you back.*
~ Arthur Rubinstein

Today is the day to celebrate. Give yourself a knowing smile, a deserved pat on the back, a little wink in the next mirror you pass. You've succeeded at making it this far—not only in the book, but in your life, too—and this is no small feat.

Consider the winding twists and curves your life has taken so far, to land you here, on the verge of another adventure. You are on the edge of personal greatness, of becoming the very best version of yourself that has ever been.

This is cause for celebration, so don't delay.

Just as you like to wait until the next day off to relax and have fun, you have a tendency to postpone your happiness until you've reached your destination, wherever that is. The problem with holding back expressing happiness until some tomorrow date is that tomorrow never comes.

After waiting for however many tomorrows to let your joy flow, the tap runs dry. You've forgotten that it was here with you, all the time. Allowing your happiness to flow, NOW, for the little victories (or even *no* reason at all, if you dare), primes the pump and gives an example of the feeling you're waiting for.

Happiness brings more happiness. You know how your smile is contagious? So is the feeling of happiness. The happier you are inside, the more happiness you see in the world outside. Awesome, right?

The journey toward a life of more happiness and less stress is one that unfolds one day at a time. Showing up happy makes the scenery more pleasant and the challenges less pressing.

The tools in this book offer a sure way into a mindset of possibility. As the feelings of stress and tension subside, the possibilities grow. You become more open, both mentally and physically.

Embracing this openness, you feel free to say, "Yes." Notice what happens when you say this word.

Yes. Or, YES! if you could be so bold.

It causes an expansion. An opening for more to flow to you.

The tension of chronic stress is like a dam, barricading the free flow of energy to and through you. Relaxation weakens this dam; celebration breaks it apart for good. Let this happiness flow like a raging river whose waters have overflowed its banks.

Celebrate your successes. Celebrate YOU.

Daily and weekly, look back at what you are proud of and acknowledge yourself. Then, take yourself out for dinner and a movie. Dance to loud music. Play with your kids. Skip down the street. Share your experience. Be an evangelist for your own happiness and watch it grow.

Every day is another opportunity to renew your commitment to you and your own happiness. No one else can do it for you.

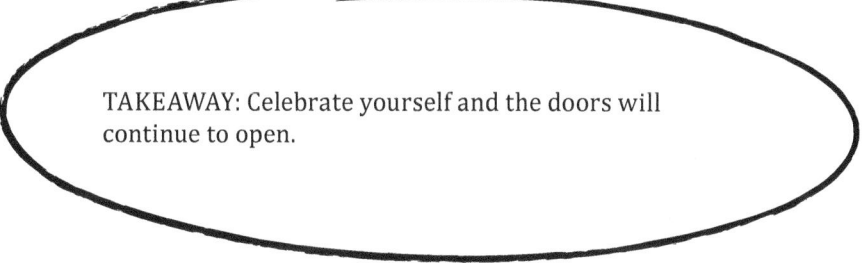

TAKEAWAY: Celebrate yourself and the doors will continue to open.

The Road Ahead

Hope is being able to see that there is light despite all of the darkness.
~ Desmond Tutu

A little more persistence, a little more effort, and what seemed hopeless failure may turn to glorious success.
~ Elbert Hubbard

It's no secret how successful people become successful; it's no secret how peaceful people deal with stress. They use tools and techniques like the ones outlined throughout this book. Their belief and their actions go hand in hand, each strengthening the other.

So often, we let others sway us from what we really want to do. We let them knock us off the path we really want to travel.

But more often than that, we're the ones who sabotage our own efforts. Regardless of how much we blame others, we are the ones who fail to manage ourselves.

Our time of excuses is over. We now have more than enough ways to reduce our stress, increase our satisfaction, and build strong relationships around us in order to get on the road to our dreams.

One bit of advice I can share with you as you contemplate the road ahead: Find an accountability partner, a coach, or mentor to work with you. When done right, dealing with your stress can be scary: It means facing fears, giving up excuses, hitting plateaus, and sometimes failing. You will run into frustrations and roadblocks; you'll try to bite off more than you can chew.

Having someone by your side whom you trust and has gone through this journey will make your steps so much easier to take. Together, you can define your goals, put a system in place, and understand when discipline is needed.

The key is small bites consistently over time.

Take the time to experiment, develop your own stress management strategy, and do what's best for you—as long as it produces positive results.

Don't worry about what other people think of you; remember, people's opinion of you is none of your business.

I challenge you to consciously decide how your life is going to be. I challenge you to commit to managing yourself so that you can have the life you want. You have all the basic tools you need to handle your stress—to succeed.

So, before you close this book, write down the one thing about your stress management that you're going to change immediately. It may be simply to count to 10 when you feel yourself getting stressed. Or maybe to do the relaxation breathing every day for a few minutes. Easy.

It's possible you've been struggling for so long with your stress, your frustration, and your exhaustion that you've come to believe that it's normal. You may doubt that the techniques presented throughout the book work.

Adam and I are living proof that they work.

The first step is believing. When you truly believe, and you face the obstacles that arise with that belief in mind, you will be able to do it.

You are more powerful than you imagine. You have the power to change your life. You hold the key to unlock every prison door you've created. Amazing things will happen when you do.

It all begins with you.

I would love to hear about your successes. You can reach me at joe@joeserio.com.

The Takeaways

Lesson 1   Burnout happens when you suppress your feelings and expect things to change without doing something different. So do something different.

Lesson 2   Burnout is driven by the stress cycles of your daily life.

Lesson 3   Knowing the forms of stress can help you deal with the challenges of your days.

Lesson 4   Unhealthy stress impacts virtually every part of your body and can be fatal.

Lesson 5   The impact of work stress on your health and mindset can be significant, especially without coping mechanisms.

Lesson 6   The reflexive way we live our lives can be harmful, but we can change.

Lesson 7   Home should be a place to recuperate from the stress of work and not exacerbate your situation.

Lesson 8   Running away from aspects of your life outside work contributes to your stress, making work life more difficult.

Lesson 9   Identify your current paradigm to find out if it's causing you stress.

Lesson 10   The beliefs you hold dictate the stress you experience.

Lesson 11   Examine your beliefs and adjust your expectations to close the gap with reality.

Lesson 12   Your values, and how you live them, play a large role in the stress you allow in your life.

Lesson 13   Priorities based on beliefs and values will guide your actions.

Lesson 14	Look deeper inside yourself to understand the causes of your anxiety.
Lesson 15	You can change your Outcomes in life by changing your Responses to the Events around you.
Lesson 16	Fight or flight can be important to your well-being, but not if it's turned on all the time.
Lesson 17	The way you tell your story matters and affects how you are now as you move into the future.
Lesson 18	Determine how the seven stress warning signs are impacting your life to see the opportunity for change.
Lesson 19	"Work" isn't necessarily stressful, just certain aspects of the job.
Lesson 20	When you take 100% responsibility for your life, you unlock your personal power.
Lesson 21	The way you think is critically important. Doing "healthy" things in a stressful way can't save you.
Lesson 22	The relaxation response is the gateway to being more Type B.
Lesson 23	Relaxing the body relaxes the mind, instantly creating the opportunity for more space.
Lesson 24	Slowing down is a powerful way to de-stress and be more connected to things that matter most.
Lesson 25	Avoidance is fear in disguise. Taking action is the surest way to banish any fear.
Lesson 26	Becoming more resilient is critical in preventing stress from taking over.
Lesson 27	What you focus on is what appears in your life.
Lesson 28	Changing what you *can* change shifts you toward opportunity and away from limitation.

Lesson 29   Do just one thing whenever you can for less distraction and less stress.

Lesson 30   Identifying your habitual thinking helps to change your thoughts and decrease your stress.

Lesson 31   Changing your thoughts changes your mood, which changes your outlook for the better.

Lesson 32   Put your inner critic in check for lasting happiness.

Lesson 33   Confidence is always accessible when you see how far you've come.

Lesson 34   Use your willpower, when you have it, to make the changes you'd most like to see.

Lesson 35   Daily hassles aren't hassles if you don't label them as such.

Lesson 36   Eat for less stress, and you'll feel less stress.

Lesson 37   Get up and get active. You'll prevent stress, stop the sitting disease, and be happier.

Lesson 38   Getting enough sleep is one of the most powerful ways to reduce stress levels.

Lesson 39   Laughter is a gateway to greater relaxation, better communication, and fun times with good people.

Lesson 40   When the people in your life support your efforts, you'll improve your life much more quickly.

Lesson 41   Forgive everyone. What they do to you isn't personal, and it only harms you to hold a grudge.

Lesson 42   Play is the key to balancing the demands of your job.

Lesson 43   Hobbies are the activities that keep you engaged with life and help you avoid burnout.

Lesson 44   Letting the spontaneous and fun-loving side of you have some fun is the surest way to find relief.

Lesson 45   Improvement in one area of your life influences all other areas.

Lesson 46   We must update our actions according to the life we want to live NOW.

Lesson 47   Knowing where you are and where you're going helps you know when you get there.

Lesson 48   Taking consistent action one step at a time is the key to quick, profound transformation.

Lesson 49   You've always known the way forward. The answers will appear if you just give them the space to. Then, take the next bold step and BE who you really are.

Lesson 50   Celebrate yourself and the doors will continue to open.

Acknowledgments

Thank you to my coworkers at the LAPD Communications Division, who participated in the early presentations and sessions that became the foundation for this book and the wellness trainings for telecommunicators that I conduct with Joe Serio. Thanks to Capt. Joel Justice for his commitment to making the Division a better place and to Lt. Vic Dennis for offering me the opportunity to speak.

Special thanks to Joe Serio for calling me out to write this book and providing the guidance and support to get it done. Our work has only just begun. Thanks also to Jennifer Serio for her meticulous eye and for all that she's done to make this possible. And thank you to Dana Lin for her unwavering belief in the vision.

Thanks to those who read the manuscript and provided feedback: Gracye Cheng, Rosanna McKinney, Hope Peyton-Wright, and Renee Anderson.

Thank you for reading this book. My hope is that these principles and tools will help you do this challenging work and thrive, every day.

— Adam Timm

My special thanks to Ivana Siska who got this ball rolling when she introduced me to Adam Timm in Los Angeles in 2013. Without that simple, "You have to meet my friend, Adam!" there would be no *Being Resilient* book. Thanks, Ivana!

Thank you to my wife, Jennifer, without whom none of this would be possible.

— Joe Serio

Biographies

Adam Timm is a retired 10-year veteran of the Los Angeles Police Department (LAPD). As a tenured 911 dispatcher for one of the busiest agencies in the country, his career threw him headlong into the debilitating effects of dispatcher stress: chronic stress from daily calls, critical incident stress from emergencies, and traumatic stress from doing it all for a decade.

After experiencing years of migraines, ulcers, and personal challenges on and off the job, he developed a step-by-step program to beat the burnout.

Adam has delivered this program to thousands of dispatchers across the country, offering powerful steps to stronger relationships, better sleep, and healthier living. His energetic and interactive speaking style engages and inspires participants.

Dr. Joe Serio is an international speaker, trainer, and author who holds a Ph.D. in Criminal Justice from Sam Houston State University (SHSU) with a specialization in Leadership and Organizational Behavior. Since 2012, Joe has been a full-time trainer and conference keynote speaker around the U.S.

Joe delivers personal leadership and wellness programs on topics such as Positive Interaction with Difficult People, Managing Fear, Emotional Intelligence, Time Management and Organizational Skills, Leadership, Customer Service, and Public Speaking for the Faint-hearted.

He is the founder and publisher of the Get the Nerve™ series of books.

In his former life, Joe was the only American to work in the Organized Crime Control Department of the Soviet National Police and later was the director of the Moscow office of the world's leading business intelligence and corporate investigation firm. He is the author of the critically acclaimed book, *Investigating the Russian Mafia*.

CPSIA information can be obtained
at www.ICGtesting.com
Printed in the USA
BVHW090712120722
641635BV00003B/13